HOW

Looking Around

Teacher's Guide

Alan Morrison

Diana Morrison

Acknowledgements

Original development work for the **Heinemann Our World** series was done by the University of Leeds Primary Curriculum Development Project.

The extracts from *Geography in the National Curriculum* are reproduced with the permission of the Controller of Her Majesty's Stationery Office.

First published 1993

Designed by Miller, Craig and Cocking
Illustrated by Jenny Partridge

Typeset by Stables Typesetting, Swindon
Printed in Great Britain by Athenaeum Press Ltd, Newcastle upon Tyne

Heinemann Educational,
a Division of Heinemann Publishers (Oxford) Ltd,
Halley Court, Jordan Hill, Oxford OX2 8EJ

OXFORD LONDON EDINBURGH
MADRID ATHENS BOLOGNA PARIS
MELBOURNE SYDNEY AUCKLAND SINGAPORE
TOKYO IBADAN NAIROBI HARARE
GABORONE PORTSMOUTH NH (USA)

CONTENTS

Introduction to HEINEMANN OUR WORLD

Heinemann Our World is an innovative topic-based approach to teaching the National Curriculum at Key Stages 1 and 2. It is designed to help you to address all the National Curriculum requirements for Geography, History, Science and Technology.

The series comprises 35 individual topics, each providing ample ideas and materials for about half a term's work. Each topic is complete in itself and can be used independently of the others. There are 12 topics focusing primarily on Geography, 8 topics focusing on History and 15 on Science and Technology.

Comprehensive coverage

To ensure that children develop the concepts and skills necessary for each subject, each topic focuses on one or two subjects. This topic focuses on Geography alone, but work in other National Curriculum core and foundation subjects and the cross-curricular themes has been integrated where appropriate.

Coverage of the National Curriculum across the topics has been carefully mapped to ensure that there is progression and variation in learning experiences and to provide ample opportunities for children to revisit key concepts. The topics for Key Stage 1 focus on Levels 1–3, with the emphasis being on Levels 1 and 2. Levels 2–5 are covered at Key Stage 2. Progression has been built into the topics focusing on Geography for Key Stage 2 as shown below:

Topic	Level
People Live Here	2, with some 3
Looking Around	2, with some 3
Our Local Community	2–3, with some 4
Here and There	3, with some 2 and 4
Where You Live	3, with some 2 and 4
Comparing Places	4, with some 3
Looking at our Environment	4, with some 3
Living in Europe	5, with some 4
The World Around You	5, with some 4

The **Heinemann Our World** materials are designed to reduce the pressures on teachers' time; through providing an integrated yet flexible approach to teaching the National Curriculum, the materials enable teachers to continue to plan and teach to meet the particular needs of their class.

Promoting skills development

Throughout the materials, children are encouraged to ask questions, to find answers for themselves and to solve problems. Many of the activities are designed to encourage children to work collaboratively. This not only helps them to acquire knowledge and concepts, but also to develop speaking, listening, cognitive and social skills.

In every topic there is a balance of activities between those requiring direction by the teacher and those that children can tackle on their own, either individually or in groups. These latter 'child-led' activities are supported by materials which can be used independently of the teacher.

Supporting the teacher

Whilst group activity work encourages children to work independently, the teacher's role is still very important. The **Teacher's Guides** give guidance on how and when teacher intervention, support and assistance might be beneficial.

In-built assessment

Assessment is continuous and fully integrated in **Heinemann Our World**. Opportunities for assessment are clearly highlighted in the **Teacher's Guides**, with the relevant **Statements of Attainment** indicated and suggestions for evidence of attainment given. Assessment is achieved through a variety of means: observation, questions and evaluation of work produced by the children.

We hope that you will enjoy using the material provided in this and other **Heinemann Our World** topics. A full list of topics is provided on page 79.

Introduction to LOOKING AROUND

Looking Around is designed to be used with 7–8 year olds (Year 3) and focuses on Level 2 of the National Curriculum, with some coverage of Level 3.

The topic focuses on Geography, but includes work in English, Maths, Science and History.

Ideas underlying the topic

- Children need to develop knowledge and understanding of the geography of where they live and of other places in the United Kingdom and abroad.

- Children should develop their geographical skills through studying places and geographical themes.

- Activities should take account of children's interests, experience and capabilities.

- Children should encounter a range of activities which are structured so that they include progression and continuity in the knowledge, skills and attitudes which the topic aims to address.

- Children benefit socially and educationally from participating in structured activities with a partner and in small groups.

- Teaching approaches and organizational strategies should suit the aims of a particular activity and should include variety.

How are these ideas provided for in this topic?

The children are asked to look at a variety of places in which people live. The relationship between the size of places and their structure is introduced at the outset, alongside the requirements that people have to live comfortably. This requires a consideration of weather and in particular the role of water, which is used as a linking theme, joining the settlements with their physical surroundings and people with their environments.

The children are asked to think about places in the British Isles (and the distinction is made between the British Isles and the United Kingdom in the teacher's handbook). Information about a variety of places in the United Kingdom is provided and contrasts are made between places with respect to settlement, size and function, the role of water, and seasonality. These factors all influence the lives of the people who live there.

Teachers are encouraged to make the children think about the differences between the places in the pupil book and where they themselves live. This may encompass cultural issues and will certainly provoke discussion about sociological ones. Thus children are introduced to a wide range of issues, some of which are followed up in *Where You Live*, in which a family is introduced to allow children to identify the role of everyday life in producing the characteristics of place. The direct experience of children through their short, frequent, exploratory trips within their own settlement and home area can be employed to good effect in discussion about the places they encounter in the book. They can also be shown how to extend their knowledge by using secondary sources.

What does the topic aim to address?

The work on **Attainment Target 1** is concerned with children's observational and analytical skills, and their use of maps and aerial photos. Opportunities are provided for:

- interpreting a variety of maps

- following and making route maps with the use of some conventional symbols

- using co-ordinates to local features on maps

- identifying urban and physical landscape features on aerial photos.

Level 2 work is reinforced through opportunities to:

- make simple representations of real and imaginary places and routes

- describe a route followed

Geography Statements of Attainment addressed in the topic

Name of Activity	Key SOAs	Other SOAs which could be assessed	Links with other subject areas
1. All alone	2/2c		
2. An island home	1/2a, 1/2e	1/2b	
3. Far from the crowds	1/2a, 1/2e	2/2c, 2/2d	
4. On the way	1/2c	1/3c	Maths, History
5. Model villages?	1/2a, 1/2e	4/3a	History
6. Changing direction	1/2c	1/3a	Maths, History
7. Finding out what's there	1/2a, 1/2e	1/3d	History
8. At the centre	1/2b	4/3b	
9. Getting around cities	1/2a, 1/2e	4/3c	Technology, History
10. Making places	4/2a		Maths, Technology
11. Putting places in their place	2/2a	2/3a, 2/3b	
12. The place of change	5/2c	5/3b	Technology, Science
13. The place of water	3/2b	3/3b	History, Science, English
14. Changing seasons: winter	3/2a, 3/2b	3/3b	English
15. Changing seasons: spring	3/2a, 3/2b	3/3b	
16. Changing seasons: summer	3/2a, 3/2b	3/3b	
17. Changing seasons: autumn	3/2a, 3/2b	3/3b	
18. Measuring the weather	1/2d		Science
19. It's raining, it's pouring	3/2b, 3/2a	3/3b	Science, Technology
20. Blow wind blow	3/2a		Maths, Art, Science, Technology
21. Just for the record	1/2d, 2/3c	1/3b	Art, Science

- identify features on photos.

Children moving to higher levels in **Attainment Target 1** will:

- start to devise symbols for use on maps
- use a key to identify features
- begin to use the index and contents pages of an atlas.

The work on **Attainment Target 2** focuses on children's knowledge of places in a national and global context. Opportunities are provided for:

- naming features located on maps of the United Kingdom and the world
- locating their local area on a map of the United Kingdom.

Children moving to higher levels will be working towards Gg1/4e by using atlases to increase their knowledge of places on national and global maps.

Attainment Target 3 work focuses on their knowledge and understanding of weather, climate and landforms. Opportunities are provided for:

- describing weather in different climatic conditions
- considering the effects of rainfall on different landscape features
- naming landscape features
- devising descriptions of landscape features.

Level 2 work is reinforced through opportunities to look at forms of water found in different weather conditions. Children moving to higher levels will be working towards Gg1/4d by beginning to measure and record weather using direct observations and simple equipment.

The work on **Attainment Target 4** focuses on their knowledge and understanding of settlements. Opportunities are provided for:

- examining some of the functions of settlements
- the development of settlements in relation to their original functions
- changes and changing functions within settlements
- examining some preferences when people move home.

Level 2 work is reinforced through opportunities to:

- examine settlements of varying sizes
- identify journeys of varying lengths
- name and describe many different locations where goods and services are obtained.

Children move to higher levels in Attainment Target 4 as they:

- identify different functions within larger settlements

- describe the land-use patterns within settlements.

The work on Attainment Target 5 focuses on their knowledge and understanding of environmental change. Opportunities are provided for:

- identifying ways of changing their environment
- describing activities which may improve the environment.

Level 2 work is reinforced through opportunities to consider some possible ways of improving the environment and changes in the use of the environment.

Children moving on to higher levels within Attainment Target 5 will begin to consider ways in which damaged areas may be improved and their function altered.

The Geography Statements of Attainment addressed in the topic are summarized in the table on page 6. Where there are opportunities for extensions into other areas of the curriculum, these have also been indicated.

Planning the use of the topic

Overview of the activities

The activities are grouped into two main topics which are considered as distinct but interrelated themes. The idea of scale is predominant in the first half of the book, which deals with settlements and their increasing complexity and range of function as size increases. The second half of the book investigates the role of water by considering its characteristics throughout the year, both in the air and when it reaches the ground. The link between the two is the control that water exerts upon the development of settlements. Although there is a progression (based on scale) throughout the book, topics can be used individually or in groups and an emphasis on a cross-curricular approach is encouraged.

Villages

In this book the examples are all taken from the United Kingdom; in subsequent books settlements from other parts of the world are used to illustrate the geographical ideas. At the outset the distinction between Great Britain and the United

Kingdom should be made. Physically the British Isles comprise England, Scotland, Wales and all of Ireland. There is no physical boundary such as a river or a mountain range to separate Ireland into Northern Ireland and Eire. The division has been made solely on political grounds. It should be pointed out to the children that settlements develop partly in response to geographical factors and partly through government intervention. The children are introduced to map types and shown how to follow routes and make plans of settlements of various sizes. The activities encourage the children to think about the changing role that villages play and to consider these functions in the light of their own experience.

Cities

The book invites children to investigate the structure and function of cities, and cites Glasgow, Cardiff and Belfast. How these functions have changed is also considered and reference is made to the role of individual buildings in cities. The problems of transport and environmental degradation which cities create are also indicated,

Overview of resources provided

Name of Activity	Relevant textbook pages	Activity Sheets	Posters
1. All Alone	4	1	
2. An island home	6	2,3	
3. Far from the crowds	8	4	
4. On the way	10	5,6	Henryd village, Wales
5. Model villages?	12	7	
6. Changing direction	14	8,9	
7. Finding out what's there	16	10	View of Conwy Castle, Wales
8. At the centre	18		Belfast, Northern Ireland
9. Getting around cities	20	11,12	
10. Making places	22		
11. Putting places in their place	24	13	
12. The place of change	26	14, 15	Mural at Mersey St. Primary School, Belfast
13. The place of water	28	16	Beach on Iona, Scotland
14. Changing seasons: winter	30	17–20	
15. Changing seasons: spring	32	17–20	
16. Changing seasons: summer	34	17–20	
17. Changing seasons: autumn	36	17–20	
18. Measuring the weather	38	21	
19. It's raining, it's pouring	40	22	
20. Blow wind blow	42		Tree uprooted in storm damage
21. Just for the record	44	23, 24	

along with some approaches these cities have adopted to overcome them. Mapping and observational skills are developed; the children explore information provided by models, maps and photographs and are introduced to the use of symbols to summarize data.

Towns

Conwy, Nairn and Crewe provide a contrast in types of town, which developed for different reasons. Crewe is the only one of the three to retain its original function. The way towns grow and change over time ('structural development based on function') is described, and activities are provided to allow children to explore this.

The reasons why people move within and between settlements are introduced. More maps and aerial photos are provided to further the children's use of these analytical tools, and increase their observational and descriptive powers.

Weather and Water

The way changes in the weather affect the form which water may take is studied through the seasons and the characteristics which they show. Factors which are considered include flora and fauna as well as weather types. The geographical vocabulary used to describe weather is introduced and the children are asked to bring their personal experience to bear on the links between weather and the environment. The small scale weather of their local area can be compared with other areas presented in the book and methods used to measure and describe rain, wind and temperature are indicated. Children are encouraged to invent their own symbols to summarize weather types and then present their data on a record sheet.

Structure and flexibility within the topic

For each activity a number of central learning opportunities drawn from the Geography Programmes of Study and the Non-Statutory Guidance have been identified. The activities have been ordered to promote continuity and progression of the knowledge, skills and attitudes addressed in the topic. You may wish to choose from the activities when planning your teaching, and perhaps devise additional activities to go alongside those suggested in this Guide.

Time

The topic can either be covered with intensive teaching in half a term, or spread over an entire term. The activities can be adapted to suit the time available. For each activity, extension, reinforcement and variation activities have been given, and the activities have been designed so that tasks can be revisited several times.

Preparing for your teaching

Resources provided

The chart on page 8 provides a summary of the materials provided for the topic. The materials comprise the pupil textbook (six copies of which are provided in Topic Starter Box), activity sheets which are included in this Guide and a poster pack.

Pupil textbook

Each spread in the textbook forms a mini-unit of work. In addition to photos, maps and easy-to-read text providing a stimulus for the activities, the spreads each have a 'Things to do' box, providing tasks for the children to do either independently or with a partner. Some of the pages give 'Detective Work' to extend the tasks further. Additional ways of extending the tasks are suggested in the activity spreads in this Guide.

On pages 46–48 of the textbook there is a glossary to help children to learn geographical vocabulary.

Activity sheets

There are 24 activity sheets. Some of these have maps of the places studied in the topic. Others provide the stimulus for follow up or extension activities. Many of the activity sheets are linked to a specific Statement of Attainment and can be used for assessment.

Poster pack

There are six full-colour posters in the pack, showing views of the places studied in the topic. They have been provided to facilitate small group discussion.

Other resources

The activities in this topic make use of resources readily found in a typical primary classroom. The following list may be helpful to you in preparing to teach the topic.

Art materials

Drawing material (e.g. wax crayons, felt pens, pencil crayons, pastels)
Scissors
White paper, drawing and ruled
Range of coloured papers and card
Graph paper
Glue, PVA and paper glue

Other materials

Tape recorder, tapes
Range of local maps: as wide a variety as possible of old and modern, and different scales (to include street maps, weather maps, tourist maps, bus, train and tube maps, Ordnance Survey maps etc.)

ACTIVITY: EACH ACTIVITY HAS A NAME AND NUMBER

Relevant pages for the pupil textbook are given in the margin.

Relevant activity sheets are given in the margin.

The photocopy symbol also appears on relevant pages of the pupil textbook.

Learning Opportunities

For each activity a number of learning opportunities are identified. These are drawn from the National Curriculum Programmes of Study and Non-Statutory Guidance.

The learning opportunities are a selection of the ones that could have been chosen.

Background Information

Information is given about the localities studied and about the geographical skills and concepts to be developed.

Teaching and Learning Notes

This section continues on the top of the following page.

Most of the activities are divided into two to four tasks. For each task details of what the task consists of are given, including advice on practical issues, how you might interact with the children and the sorts of ideas that the children will need to consider.

Extensions and Variations

This section provides suggestions on how you might extend the activity both geographically and cross-curricularly.

Assessment opportunities	Statements of Attainment	Evidence of attainment	Bases of assessment
For each activity **Key SoAs** and **Other SoAs which could be assessed** are given.	Written out in full for your convenience.	What to look for to judge whether the child has achieved this SoA.	How the assessment is done, e.g. Oral.

Photos of features in the local area, different
    types of transport and goods and services
Range of local information brochures
Street directories for local area
Yellow Pages and other trade directories
Local and national newspapers
Compasses
Counters
Postcards
Labels from food tins
Atlases
Rain gauge
Thermometer

Preparing your classroom

Throughout the topic the children will be
producing material which can be used to create
an evolving display. This display can be
enhanced by the addition of material collected
by you or the children.

Some suggestions of things to collect are
given below:

- any material available from your local
  Tourist Information Office

- maps of the local area in a range of sizes
  and scales (large scale maps and aerial
  photos are often available from the local

council's planning department)

- travel agents' brochures on holidays in the
  United Kingdom

- postcards, artefacts and tourist information
  from other regions.

Ideas for sharing the topic

At the end of the topic, you and the children may
wish to share the information you have learned
with others. Your audience could be other
children in the school, the head teacher or
parents or other people from the community.

The methods used to share the information
with others could be equally varied. You could:

- invite people to the classroom to see the
  displays

- put up a display elsewhere (e.g. sometimes
  local building societies and other shops
  allow schools to put up displays in their
  windows)

- put on a presentation, either during an
  assembly or elsewhere

- write books about the places studied.

Assessment

The chart on page 10 explains the design of the
activity spreads. As can be seen, the assessment
opportunities for each task have been clearly
indicated.

We have identified the assessment
opportunities and *how* you can assess. *When*
you assess the children and *who* you assess
(i.e. whether you assess children in a group or
individually) has been left open, so that you can
choose the time and group size which best suits
your children, your way of teaching and the
purposes of your assessment.

For example, formative or on-going

assessments of the children's work can be made
to decide whether a child needs more
experience of an activity or needs a different
type of activity.

If you are making a summative assessment
you may decide to do so after a child has had a
number of opportunities to consolidate her/his
learning.

A summary of the Statements of Attainment
addressed in the topic is provided on page 6.

Your school or LEA may have already
produced a record-keeping chart. Alternatively,
you can use the one on page 78.

ACTIVITY 1: ALL ALONE

Learning Opportunities

There are opportunities for developing the understanding, skills and attitudes involved in:

▲ appreciating how people communicate with each other

▲ looking at the different requirements for living

▲ looking at other places where people live

Background Information

Places are characterized by distinctive features. Children's knowledge of place is gained in two ways, either from first-hand experience gained through exploration and contact, or from media information which tends to be selective. Within their local area children travel frequently and build a detailed picture of its geography, whereas for distant places their picture depends upon selected images portrayed on television, radio, in comics, or from a few short visits like holidays. The characteristics of a place are often summarized by a single feature. Paris is summed up by a picture of the Eiffel Tower, London by Buckingham Palace.

There is a wide variety of settlements in the United Kingdom, some with single buildings, some with a few buildings, and so on to urban areas which are so completely built up that only buildings can be seen. The nature of a place is also influenced by its physical characteristics, including weather, landscape, lakes, rivers and vegetation. We return to this later in the book. Rivers, coasts and lakes or other water margins form landscapes of persistent appeal and for this reason they are used as images on postcards.

Encourage the children to think of the landscape they like the most and then ask them about the physical factors which would make living there alone difficult. How would they ensure they had warmth and shelter as well as food and water? Remote places such as the one in the photo, if they are threatening or inhospitable, are described as 'topophobic'. Places which are enjoyable to be in (and may also be remote) are described as 'topophilic'. Section 1 focuses on how places have features which make them individual and how people who live in these places or visit them on holiday value this individuality.

Assessment opportunities
KEY SoA: Gg2/2c

Statements of Attainment
Identify features of a locality outside the local area and suggest how these might affect the lives of the people who live there

---

Teaching and Learning Notes

1, 2 & 3 In remote areas there may be few services to provide for a comfortable or safe existence — there may be no doctor, or no supermarket. The bare necessities for life have to be brought in to the remote area; so do other items which, while not essential, make living more enjoyable. Let the children make up their own lists. It may be too short, or contain some less than essential items, but they will be using their own experience. The word square contains some items which are necessary and some which are simply comfort providing, and it may be helpful if the children place them into these two categories as they find them. Some of the items (such as trees or water) are part of the natural landscape. Others (like stars, which are important for navigation) will not be seen as immediately useful by the children. When the items have been found and sorted, the lists can be compared, and the comparison can form the basis for group discussions. The lists can be re-grouped under other headings, for instance 'natural' and 'manufactured'.

Extensions and Variations

On Activity Sheet 1: *Send a postcard*, the children have to identify which features could best convey in pictorial form the nature of a place with which they are familiar. Consider beforehand whether the child considers natural or built features to be more important. There is no 'right' answer to this. The usefulness of the exercise lies in the children's recognizing landmarks which have most impressed them. There is also the opportunity to develop geographical vocabulary in describing the features which have been chosen, particularly those in the local area. The message the children add to the postcard should suggest what sort of a place is described by the feature(s) chosen. For instance, the message from a remote place might be 'Just getting away from it all'. The activity also reinforces Gg 2/1c.

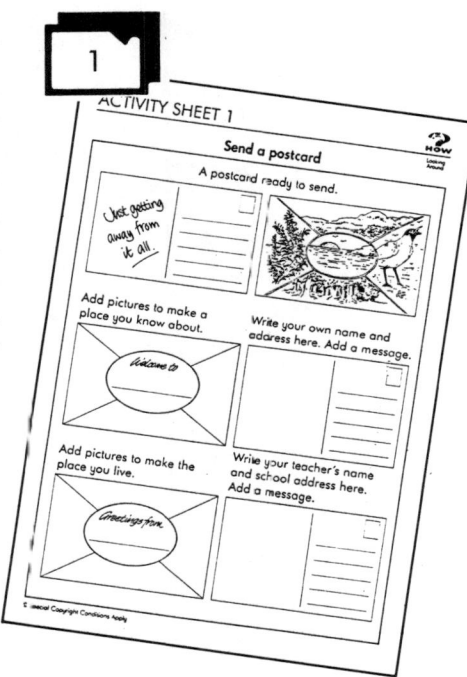

Evidence of attainment

Child draws a picture of an imaginary place. By completing the address on the card, the child will also be fulfilling Gg2/1c

Bases of assessment

Product

ACTIVITY 2:   AN ISLAND HOME

Learning Opportunities

There are opportunities for children to develop the understanding, skills and attitudes involved in:

▲   making drawings of maps of a real place

▲   investigating the different ways that people keep in touch

▲   finding out how symbols are used on maps

Background Information

There are still some areas of the British Isles which can be considered remote even though they can be reached by rail or road within a day, or directly by telephone. Parts of the west coast of Scotland are remote and in these areas crofting – the traditional way of subsisting from the environment – is still sometimes practised. Crofting involves farming and fishing, and traditionally the produce grown and caught were used to feed the family and were not sold for money. Which crops were grown was dictated by the weather (high rainfall, short warm summer), and consequently consisted of hay, oats, and root vegetables. These fed both the livestock and the people. The hay rick visible in the photograph in the pupil book illustrates the way the hay was stored over the winter. Herring were the chief fish caught, and these were preserved by being salted or smoked (kippered) for eating during the winter, when bad weather makes fishing hazardous. Lobsters and crabs were also caught and these could be sent to cities for sale because of the high prices they would fetch; some crofters caught salmon in sea nets just offshore – a high income product but with a limited season. As time passed, traditional industries undertaken by the crofters to provide clothes and ornaments for themselves became famous as craft industries and found markets with tourists and in the towns and cities throughout the rest of the United Kingdom. So the traditional subsistence life-style gave way to earning money by selling those goods and crafts which had developed from the way of life of the community. Nowadays this type of 'cottage industry' has taken over from farming. People move away in search of an easier way of life, and many of the crofts now lie empty.

Assessment opportunities	*Statements of Attainment*
KEY SoAs: Gg1/2a	Use geographical vocabulary to talk about places
Gg1/2e	Identify familiar features on photographs and pictures
Other SoA which could be assessed:	
Gg1/2b	Make a representation of a real or imaginary place

Teaching and Learning Notes

1 Making a map

Sketch maps are a useful way of representing real places in a simplified manner. They show the main features – buildings, roads, railways, rivers, but no vegetation or relief. In this activity the children have to interpret the map and select an appropriate colour which makes the detail easier to follow. Activity Sheet 2: *Sketch map of Iona* can be used here. It is probably a good idea to discuss what a good colour would be and why – the children can do this in groups. Neatness is important, so that the detail on the maps does not become obscured. Are there things missing on the island map which they would find in their local area?

2 Finding out about places

Geographers use a variety of sources to find out about places. In the pupil book various methods have been suggested. Pooling ideas may enable the children to think of some more. The picture is there to help initiate discussion. Direct the children towards atlases, textbooks, travel guides etc.

Extensions and Variations

The children could be encouraged to write letters to imaginary people in distant places in the UK, e.g., an island in Scotland, describing what it is like where they live and asking questions about where the person in the distant place lives. What sort of questions should be asked? You will need to offer guidance with this!

Activity Sheet 2 is an enlarged version of the *Sketch map of Iona* and can be used to help children to familiarize themselves further with the use of symbols on maps. In groups they could decide which features are described by the symbols and then compile a list of the features which are found on Iona. This will lead on to Activity Sheet 3: *Comparing Iona with near my school*, in which then children have to identify features on Iona and near their school. These are placed in the appropriate part of the Carroll diagram so that the features listed which are found only in Iona are placed in the top row of the diagram, and those from only the local area are put in the left-hand column. Any common to both are placed in the overlapping top left-hand corner. This will create a visual picture of the differences and similarities between the places and allow children to classify features.

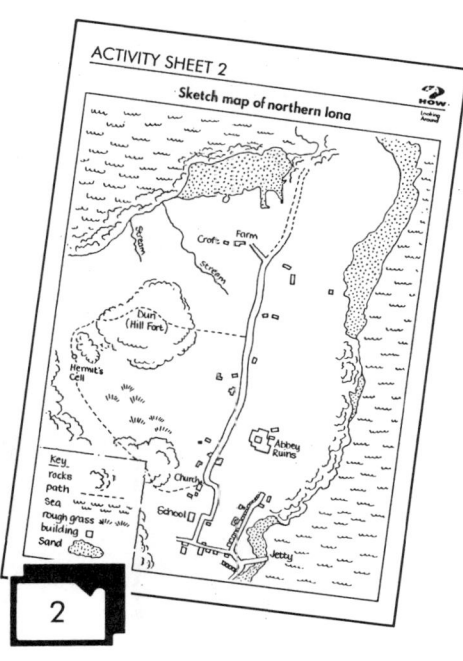

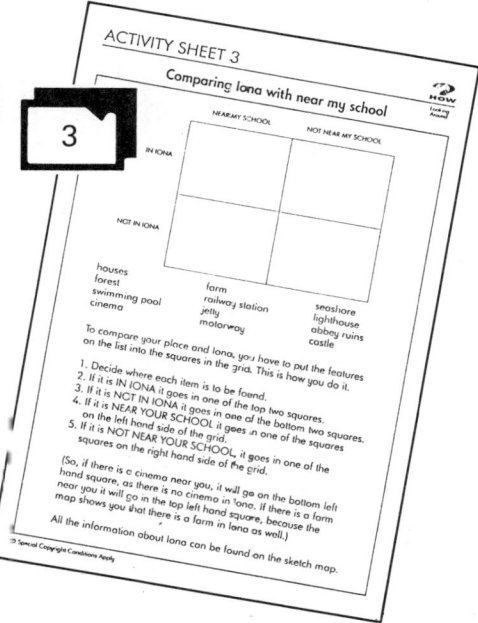

Evidence of attainment	*Bases of assessment*
Child uses geographical vocabulary in talking about a place	Oral
Child identifies features from a picture or photo	Oral
Child makes a drawing or picture of a real or imaginary place	Product

ACTIVITY 3: FAR FROM THE CROWDS

Learning Opportunities

There are opportunities for children to develop the understanding, skills and attitudes involved in:

▲ identifying features which may be familiar to them, using photos and pictures

▲ using geographical words to talk about the places they see

▲ describing different natural landscapes

▲ identifying natural features in the landscape

Background Information

Three contrasting areas have been featured in this spread, and the differences arise from the underlying geology, with the hardest, oldest rocks found in the western side of the British Isles producing the highest, steepest landscape. The area around Laxton is very flat, with deep fertile soils and the local weather promotes the growth of cereal crops. The field size is very large to allow bigger machines to be used, because this is more efficient in terms of modern farming practice. The removal of hedgerows has given rise to soil erosion and other environmental problems.

The second landscape described is Snowdonia where the land is very steep and the soils are thin and not very rich. This is partly due to the action of glaciers, which, ten thousand years ago, scraped the soil and loose rock from the surface of the land and deposited it in the east and south regions of the British Isles. Since then soil development has been slow in these cool, wet areas. Farms tend to be small and concentrate on grazing for animals, which means that fields too are small to allow the animals to be collected easily. Often the farms are on hillsides.

In between these two agricultural extremes, are the 'downlands' which are characterized by rolling hills, with valleys frequently winding through the landscape and moderately deep and fertile soils. Although the weather would allow cereal crops to be extensively grown, the hilly landscape prevents the use of large machines. Crops are therefore grown on the lower slopes of the hills, while the steeper land higher up is used for grazing. In Snowdonia, by contrast, there is very little vegetation for grazing above 1000 metres and the weather is so harsh that animals have to be fed indoors in winter. However the downland and highland areas tend to be more scenically interesting. Tourism is now a major industry, sometimes more important than farming.

Assessment opportunities	Statements of Attainment
KEY SoAs: Gg1/2a	Use geographical vocabulary to talk about places
Gg1/2e	Identify familiar features on photographs and pictures
Other SoAs which could be assessed:	
Gg2/2c	Identify features of a locality outside the local area and suggest how these might affect the lives of the people who live there
Gg2/2d	Describe similarities and differences between the local area and another locality specified in the programme of study

Teaching and Learning Notes

1 Spotting the differences

The pictures are very different and the task of finding a variety of landscape features will help the children to think about the differences that exist in the United Kingdom. Observation in geography is very important and geographers rely heavily on pictures or maps which contain a large amount of information.

Children may not be familiar with abstracting information from such sources, particularly aerial or oblique aerial photographs. Magnifying glasses may be necessary to find some of the features. This also introduces the idea of scale – houses, which are of recognizable proportions, provide a constant reference when pictures of landscape are being studied.

2 Recognizing landmarks

The matter of observation is extended in the second task which requires children to find features for themselves without the aid of a list. They should use the suggestions in the first task and then see how they can extend them.

3 Matching the right words to the places

Geographical language is important in describing landscape and many of the words will be familiar. Some help may be required initially to identify some of the features. Children may wonder why there is no river in the Laxton picture. The reasons are twofold: there are no hills locally where rain might collect in a stream and there would need to be higher rainfall and larger slopes for rivers to flow in this area.

Extensions and Variations

Activity Sheet 4: *My special place* encourages the children to recall special places where they have been or would like to go to be far from the crowds. Thus children are encouraged to think about choosing items to summarize a place, much in the same way as a postcard does. The chest is a physical expression of memory and the items may be of a geographical nature. Feeling away from it all and being away from it all are not the same thing and this is a useful but quite difficult distinction to make.

Evidence of attainment	Bases of assessment
Child creates sentences using the appropriate vocabulary	Product
Child identifies the features in the photos from the list	Oral/Product
Child identifies features in photos, e.g. lack of river in Photo A, and talks about how this affects farming there	Oral
Child compares places in photos with local areas	Oral

ACTIVITY 4:   ON THE WAY

Learning Opportunities

There are opportunities for children to develop the understanding, skills and attitudes involved in:

▲ following a route by using a plan of a place

▲ realizing that different buildings are used for different purposes

▲ drawing a map of a short route, showing certain features in order

Background Information

Henryd is a small village a couple of miles inland from Conwy in north Wales. There is an old centre to the village with a chapel and village hall forming the original nucleus. It is likely that the village grew up around the chapel and became sufficiently large to support a school, which has been recently extended. There have been recent additions to the village, namely a council estate and a private estate with some other houses added in the spaces alongside the road. Although the village has grown in size the village shop has closed down. The post office now opens only on Thursdays to provide pensions; shopping is done in the supermarkets of Conwy.

The tasks will introduce the children to a simple map which is the basic source of geographical information and allow them to make the connection between the real world as shown in photos and the abstract view of the map. In addition real buildings are shown in photos on the map to allow the children to locate them themselves. The tasks will also emphasize the variety of buildings and their uses, and illustrates the dearth of shops and entertainment in remoter rural places.

Teaching and Learning Notes

1 Finding the way around

Finding your way around the built environment is not an easy task and the children must start at the correct place, i.e., the bridge, otherwise the instructions will not make sense. The children should discuss the buildings that can be seen on the photo (page 10) and try to relate this to the map.

Remember that the orientation of the photo and the map are different, as is the representation of scale. This is why it is useful in following a route to give instructions related to clear landmarks or obvious types of buildings. Many maps (the London Underground is a good example) are very simple in their representation to help people find their way around, and do not represent the complex layout that actually exists.

Assessment opportunities	Statements of Attainment
KEY SoAs: Gg1/2c	Follow a route using a plan
Other SoA which could be assessed:	
Gg1/3c	Make a map of a short route, showing features in the correct order

2 The route in reverse

Children of this age will find it difficult to reverse a route in their head and so the activity encourages them to physically turn around (by turning the book) and see which buildings are now on their left and right using the hands to provide an initial prompt. The reality has not changed but their view of it has.

3 Identifying features

Children can be asked what the particular features are that allowed them to recognize a building as a school or a chapel or a shop. Are there some features that all shops or schools have? Which buildings could they use most easily to describe their route? They can discuss this in small groups.

Extensions and Variations

Activity Sheet 5: *Things to see in Henryd, Wales* asks children to pair up the pictures of buildings or parts of the village with items which could be found in or on them. This develops the idea of function of buildings and opens the question of what constitutes a village. Activity Sheet 6: *On the way* is a blank map to allow the children to produce a map of a route in their local area. This could be from home to school, or from home to the shops and it employs the same principle as the original activity. It should not be a map of the actual buildings on the ground, but a route map showing the sequence in which certain buildings are passed. It will give the children the basis for the ideas of direction, perspective, location, scale and the use of symbols which they will need to understand by the end of their time in primary school. Because of their more frequent journeys in the local area their image of the route followed from one place to another may be clearer than in the example of Henryd.

Activities can also be extended to include Maths and History. There are several reasons why villages grow up in the places that they do. They may be near a castle (protection) as Conwy, by the bridging point of a river (strategic), or as a market centre (geographical), by a shrine (religious), or a combination of several of these. The more numerous the reasons, the larger the settlement; often the original reasons have declined in importance, or been superseded by others (e.g., ease of commuting).

Evidence of attainment	Bases of assessment
Child follows the route correctly identifying the buildings in order	Observation/Product
Child makes a route map of their local area with buildings correctly identified	Product

ACTIVITY 5:   MODEL VILLAGES?

Learning Opportunities

There are opportunities for children to develop the understanding, skills and attitudes involved in:

▲   discussing familiar features about places

▲   making observational drawings of villages from photographic material

▲   talking about the different roles that settlements play

Background Information

There are three contrasting types of villages looked at in this section; although once they all were farming villages, the Irish village is now the only one to retain its original purpose. Both Bourton on the Water and Eaglesham have developed along different lines. Eaglesham represents one of the most common modern uses of villages, namely as a base for commuting. Commuting to work on a large scale began in the 1960s and has grown steadily since. It has engendered rapid growth in housing but seldom any improvement in services. This is because most commuters travel and shop by car. They do try, on the whole, to preserve the villages as they appeared in the past and tend to be opposers of new building or development.

Bourton is an example of a village now almost entirely supported by the tourist industry attracted by the picturesque nature of the buildings and the materials from which they are constructed and the stream which runs through the middle of the village. As a result there are many more services but not all of them are of much use to the residents, because they are designed to supply the tourist industry. Glenoe, in Northern Ireland, has fewest services despite carrying out a much more functional purpose in supporting a working farming community. This paradox can be discussed with the children. Discussion will be especially appropriate where they feel that their settlement fits within the range described above. They should be encouraged to talk about familiar features found in the place where they live, and through discussion the level of their observations can be noted.

Assessment opportunities   *Statements of Attainment*

KEY SoAs: Gg1/2a   Use geographical vocabulary to talk about places

             Gg1/2e   Identify familiar features on photographs and pictures

Other SoA which could be assessed:

             Gg4/3a   Give reasons why people change their home

Teaching and Learning Notes

1 Identifying buildings

This task is designed to make the children look closely at sets of data and interpret what is contained within them. It also introduces the idea of creating a different representation of a real feature: the sketch is a simplified version of the photo and is one step towards creating a map which is a type of model of reality.

2 Comprehension

This is a simple exercise which quickly assesses whether the child can distinguish between the different functions the villages have and relate them to the village type.

3 Shopping list

This task asks children to draw a picture of one of the villages. After they have done so the pictures (and villages) could be compared. Choose a service with which they will be familiar, e.g. shops. Make a list of the shops that would be found in each of the villages and decide which ones are found in all of them.

Extensions and Variations

Village living affects different age groups in different ways. To bring this out Activity Sheet 7: *Reasons to move* shows a series of drawings which have to be matched. The children must decide which people belong to the buildings shown and which speech bubbles explain why. This requires the children to understand the function of buildings and the needs of different groups. It also suggests that people may be able to move within their own village rather than moving away from the area. The children should be encouraged in discussion to relate their own experiences and knowledge of their own place to the situations shown in the spread. This provides an introduction to Gg4/3a and Gg4/3b, a theme pursued in *Where We Live*. There are also links with History. Further insight might be gained if an older person from a family who have lived for several generations in the same place could come to the school and talk to the children about life when they were young and the changes that have taken place since then.

Evidence of attainment	Bases of assessment
Child uses geographical terms correctly in discussion	Oral
Child recognizes and identifies features on photos and pictures	Oral/Observation
Child gives reasons why people might want to change where they live	Oral

ACTIVITY 6: CHANGING DIRECTION

Learning Opportunities

There are opportunities for children to develop the understanding, skills and attitudes involved in:

▲ following a route using a plan

▲ using geographical vocabulary to discuss features on a map

Background Information

This spread reinforces and extends the pupils by ranging across three levels at Attainment Target 1. The children will need to follow directions, but unlike the left, right, forward, back instructions of spread no 4.(On the Way) they will use compass points and co-ordinates to locate the features on the map. These techniques allow them to follow a route but in a more sophisticated way.

The town chosen as the example is Nairn on the Moray Firth in north east Scotland. Originally a small fishing port, it has grown subsequently because of its position as the lowest bridging point on the River Nairn, and as the market town for the surrounding area. The original houses of the Fishertown can be seen as a distinct area around the harbour. The fish caught were herring and some of the houses in the Fishertown had a smoke shed built next to the house to smoke the fish (making kippers) which were then sent to nearby towns and even cities such as Glasgow. Every small port on the Moray Firth and along the east coast of Scotland had its small fleet of fishing boats, but eventually the towns with better harbours which could let bigger boats into them grew in importance and the boats from the nearby ports moved to these new bases. Peterhead, just a few miles east of Nairn, is now the major fishing port in the north east of Scotland, and Aberdeen has become more important as a base for the oil industry. The harbour at Nairn has become a marina with the emphasis on sailing for pleasure; the old Fishertown has remained virtually intact with the houses looking the same as they did a hundred years ago. The local farming community which grows cereal crops and beef cattle with sheep on the higher ground inland comes to Nairn for its services.

Whereas the Fishertown has no street plan – the houses were just built where people wanted them – the rest of Nairn has a structured appearance and this is the basis of the map for the children to follow. The two stages of the town's development are reflected in the buildings and features found there. These reflect the importance and the size of the settlement as the children will find out by following their way around the route.

Assessment opportunities

KEY SoA: Gg1/2c

Statements of Attainment

Follow a route using a plan

Other SoA which could be assessed:

Gg1/3a

Use letter/number co-ordinate to locate features on a map

Teaching and Learning Notes

1 Following directions

The exercise provides an introduction to the use of map squares, initially by asking the child to follow directions based on compass notation, ie. north, east, south and west ('Never Eat Shredded Wheat' is one way of remembering the compass points in the right order; perhaps the children can think of others). The child pauses to identify the position on the map and then moves an exact distance in the appropriate direction to a new location. This operation is repeated until the journey is completed.

2 Features of a town

In addition to following directions the children have to recognize features from the map and then construct a sentence which will provide a check on their accuracy. Thus the child becomes familiar with basic geographical skills, namely following compass directions, assessing scale and identifying the features found in towns on a map.

Extensions and Variations

A natural extension, and one which leads to level 4 geographical skills, is to use a similar grid but this time with no map. On Activity Sheet 8: *Changing direction* pupils must locate themselves in space (ie, on the grid) and follow the instruction which requires them to identify a direction and complete a task in that area. This reinforces the previous exercise and it is easy to assess the children's understanding on completion.

A further refinement is for pairs of children to play a game similar to 'Battleships', using Activity Sheet 9: *Find the houses* Each child needs a copy of the Activity Sheet. Without showing their partner, they should locate a square and mark 'H' for 'house' in it. They then have to find which square each other's houses are on by suggesting co-ordinates, then recording on their sheet whether they were correct or not.

This activity can be linked to Mathematics, eg, discussing changes in size of settlements, and the increased number of buildings and features in the town compared with the village. In addition the historical changes which have been identified can be talked about, as a first step towards discussing change in the local area.

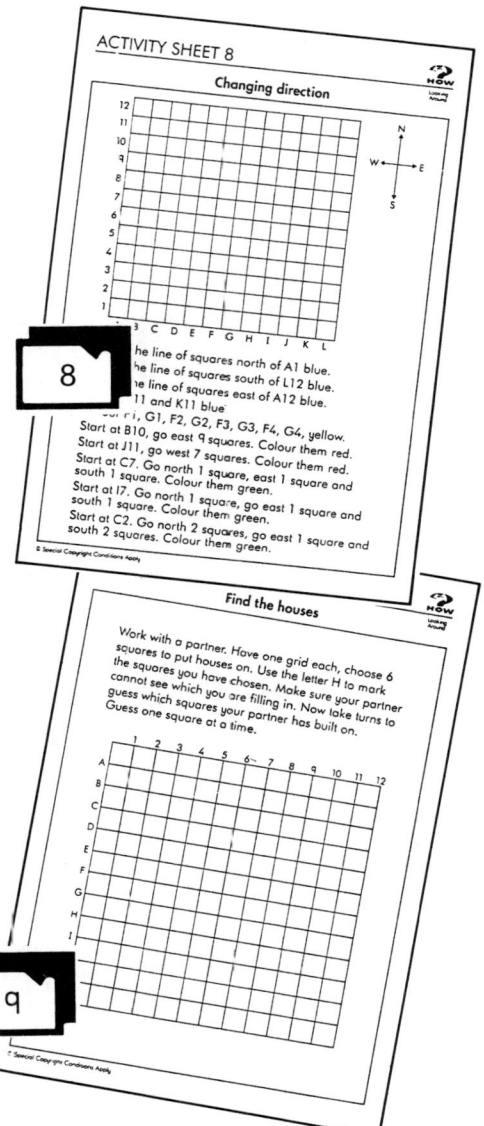

Evidence of attainment

Child follows the route and creates the sentence

Child correctly identifies the features on the map squares, using the numbers and letters

Bases of assessment

Product

Observation

Learning Opportunities

There are opportunities for children to develop the understanding, skills and attitudes involved in:

▲   talking about a familiar place

▲   using geographical vocabulary to talk about places

▲   identifying features from aerial and other photographs

Background Information

Settlements take on a different appearance when viewed from above or when represented in pictorial form. As they grow in size, they also increase in complexity with a larger range of buildings and services being offered in cities and towns than in villages. The purpose of this exercise is to identify some of the main features which are found in towns and to enable pupils to find things by studying pictures of towns taken from above which are not quite full aerial pictures. Using symbols with words underneath introduces the idea of a key. This is important in any geographical study, because where maps are used a key is always needed to explain the symbols used. The symbols on maps remain constant, even when the scale changes, though additional symbols may be used on larger scale maps, whereas on maps of smaller scale detail and symbols are fewer. It is important to make the connection between size, services and the problem of finding your way about.

Large towns are often characterized by a salient feature or industry, so that Conwy is known for its castle (and probably also its tunnel), whilst Crewe is most famous for its rail industry, or as the home of Rolls Royce motor cars. Conwy grew up as a fortified town adjoining a castle which held houses within its extensive walls. The town dates from the 13th century when Edward I, attempting to subdue the Welsh, built a number of castles in North Wales. It is also the lowest bridging point on the river Conwy and a small fishing port, mostly used by pleasure boats nowadays. Crewe is unusual in that the town was deliberately chosen as a place for growth: before 1860 it was just a village but rapid growth followed the decision by the Grand Junction Railway to develop it as a rail centre complete with engineering works. Consequently Crewe grew in a highly structured and planned manner in contrast to Nairn (especially the Fishertown) and Conwy.

Assessment opportunities	Statements of Attainment
KEY SoAs: Gg1/2a	Use geographical vocabulary to talk about places
Gg1/2e	Identify familiar features on photographs and pictures
Other SoA which could be assessed:	
Gg1/3d	Identify features on aerial photographs

Teaching and Learning Notes

1 Features of towns

The aim of the picture alphabet is to encourage the children to think of all the features that may be found in towns using letters of the alphabet to help them. They may need some guidance to ensure that the features they identify are things that would be found in a town. There is an opportunity for some brainstorming, or the children may prefer to start off working on their own.

2 A closer look

The aim here is to improve observation and to familiarize the children with photographs of towns taken from above street level. It can be pointed out that some features become more obvious from a higher viewpoint, whilst others are less easily seen. Reinforcement comes through relating what the children see to the alphabet in the previous exercise.

Extensions and Variations

Activity Sheet 10: *Finding out what's there* builds on the work the children have done on the photo; the line drawing is an enlargement of the photo and introduces another representation of a town. Pupils should be able to identify the features and recognize the change of scale, but the purpose of the activity is to introduce the idea of the function of a settlement. The boxes should be filled in with the name of the feature indicated by the arrow and these should be discussed in turn. The children should be asked to think of reasons why these features are important in the historical development of Conwy. The castle was a necessary protection and the people chose to build their houses inside its walls. The bridge was an important crossing point on the river to allow traffic from north Wales and Anglesey to travel to north west England. The harbour grew to accommodate the import and export of goods in addition to supporting a local fishing industry. The houses provide shelter for the people who were attracted to the area as a result of the previous features. These functions changed through time: with the opening of the tunnel in 1991 the road bridge has become less important than previously. Discuss this point with the children and explain that for some towns which did not have a variety of functions the town stopped growing when its single function was no longer vital to the area. This is particularly true of industries which depended on a finite local natural resource. This relates to Gg4/3b and Gg4/2a with linkages to the History curriculum.

Evidence of attainment	Bases of assessment
Child talks about a settlement using geographical language	Oral
Child identifies a variety of buildings and structures related to settlements	Oral
Child recognizes the features on the aerial photos	Oral

ACTIVITY 8: AT THE CENTRE

Learning Opportunities

There are opportunities for children to develop the understanding, skills and attitudes involved in:

▲ using geographical words to talk about features found in cities

▲ investigating the different uses to which buildings are put

▲ drawing a picture of their own school building

Background Information

Cities are important for the services and shops which are found there; some cities are important as centres which also provide the government for the country. Each of the countries of the United Kingdom has its own capital and London contains Parliament where laws affecting the whole of the UK are passed. The capital is not always the largest city in a country (Edinburgh is smaller than Glasgow). Over the last ten years there has been a tendency for people to move out of the old industrial cities of the UK into the surrounding rural areas. In addition many industries and factories have moved onto 'green field' sites, partly because improved technology has brought better communication with national centres. Belfast represents an old industrial city which is also the capital city of Northern Ireland. The city grew around the port which was an important cotton-weaving centre, but suffered from having to import machinery and raw materials from Scotland and eventually could not compete with Glasgow. The factories changed to making high-quality linen cloth; now this cloth has been largely replaced by nylon and other artificial fibres. Other industries for which Belfast was also famous include shipbuilding, engineering and aircraft manufacturing. There are consequently a wide range of buildings, some of which are shown in the pupil book. The use of buildings is constantly changing, as frequently happens in cities. The cost of suitable land (i.e., central, with all the necessary services already in place) is high so it is cheaper to buy and alter old buildings than build new ones. Some buildings, such as schools, churches, supermarkets,

Assessment opportunities

KEY SoA: Gg1/2b

Other SoA which could be assessed:

Gg4/3b

Statements of Attainment

Make a representation of a real or an imaginary place

Identify features of settlements which reveal their functions or origins

show by their shape what they were built for. Can the children think of any others? The buildings in the centre of a city are often full of people during the day but empty at night. Recently, some handsome, old buildings (warehouses, for example) in ports like Liverpool and Cardiff have been adapted internally to make housing, and the central spaces of the city have been reoccupied.

Teaching and Learning Notes

1 Cities provide services

People carry out a wide range of activities in cities, many more than are found in towns or villages. People may come to the city for jobs, and some of these jobs are services: they provide financial advice, medical care, help with holidays and so on, as well as places for eating and drinking on special occasions.

The people in the pictures are involved in social activities as well as work and this is a point to make. The size of cities means that there are more people in one place to spend money and so some things are cheaper than they would be in a village shop. Entertainment centres, such as cinemas need a lot of customers to be used fully and in a village there may not be enough people to keep them busy.

2 Your own school

From the children's own experience of school, they can see how many different jobs and different people are needed to keep a school running.

3 All shapes and sizes

There are likely to be a variety of buildings near the school, and the children can discuss how the function of a building can be recognized (whether by a sign or its shape or a combination of the two). From there let them explore the uses that buildings are put to and the need to design different buildings for different purposes. Encourage them to think of reasons why the buildings have been built in the shapes they have.

Evidence of attainment	*Bases of assessment*
Child draws a picture of their school	Product
Child writes a sentence about a feature or building in a settlement describing what its function is	Product

ACTIVITY 9: GETTING AROUND CITIES

Learning Opportunities

There are opportunities for children to develop the understanding, skills and attitudes involved in:

▲ talking about cities using geographical vocabulary

▲ using photographs to identify familiar objects and features

▲ deciding why some cities are located where they are

Background Information

There are two large cities used in the pupil book, Cardiff (a capital city) and Glasgow (a major Scottish city). Both are ports on the western coast of the UK, and initially relied on trade with the Americas for their growth. Both had industries based on coal and steel: Cardiff exported coal (which was used by steamships) and sheet metal, while Glasgow, which imported cotton, tobacco and sugar, used coal to produce steam for textile mills. They have both declined in importance as ports, partly because modern large ships require deeper water and partly because most trade is now with Europe. Both these cities were built on rivers at the nearest bridging points to the sea. (This is a common reason for building a town which may then grow into a city.) In addition both cities have undergone revitalization in recent years through different agencies; Glasgow used a Garden Festival site as a springboard to bring in new industries and money, whereas Cardiff has invested in a redevelopment of the docks including a barrage across Cardiff Bay. The traditional industries have given way to service-type industries. The city population combines to provide a large pool of labour and a market for consumer goods. There are two important ideas here which are studied by geographers, namely, that to survive economically, cities must either meet a specific need ('specialize') or a range of requirements ('diversify').

Teaching and Learning Notes

1 Getting about (signs and symbols)

The children need to be aware of the variety of transport available in the city and some of the effects this has on the city's appearance. The photograph of the bridges underlines the importance of a crossing point on the river. The Glasgow Underground is one way for people to move about. The exercise also shows that for people to move around cities easily, information must be accessible. Where space is in short supply, symbols may be used to locate where a feature can be found.

Assessment opportunities	*Statements of Attainment*
KEY SoAs: Gg1/2a	Use geographical vocabulary to talk about places
Gg1/2e	Identify familiar features on photographs and pictures
Other SoA which could be assessed:	
Gg4/3c	Explain why different forms of transport are used

2 Rivers

Exchanging ideas is important at any level of learning and in this activity the children are encouraged to discuss reasons for locating cities on the sites where they are found. They may require some directing in this activity – why should some settlements grow larger than others for example? It may be useful for children to work in pairs and for you to record their ideas on a black/white board so that all the class can see the different ideas that are produced.

Extensions and Variations

The table on Activity Sheet 11: *Transport to and from Glasgow* provides a summary of a major function of the city, namely to have a very well developed transport system to allow people to move in and out as easily as possible. Using the words and phrases given the children should complete the table to show types of transport, the type of terminus (e.g. station, ferry port, airport or car park), and the physical features that determine where that type of transport should be placed. This extends the pupils' activity into level 3, specifically Gg4/3d, but provides no more than a taster for them to refer to in the future. It also reinforces the idea of functions of settlements in this case by focusing on transport.

Activity Sheet 12: *Where to cross* picks up on the problem of crossing a river which has been mentioned in the pupil book. Although bridges enable people in cars, lorries, buses, trains, bicycles and on foot to cross a river they are not the only, or even necessarily the best, way of getting across. Can the children identify the appropriate method in the four situations described in the Activity Sheet? This encourages the use of geographical vocabulary and has links with technology and history.

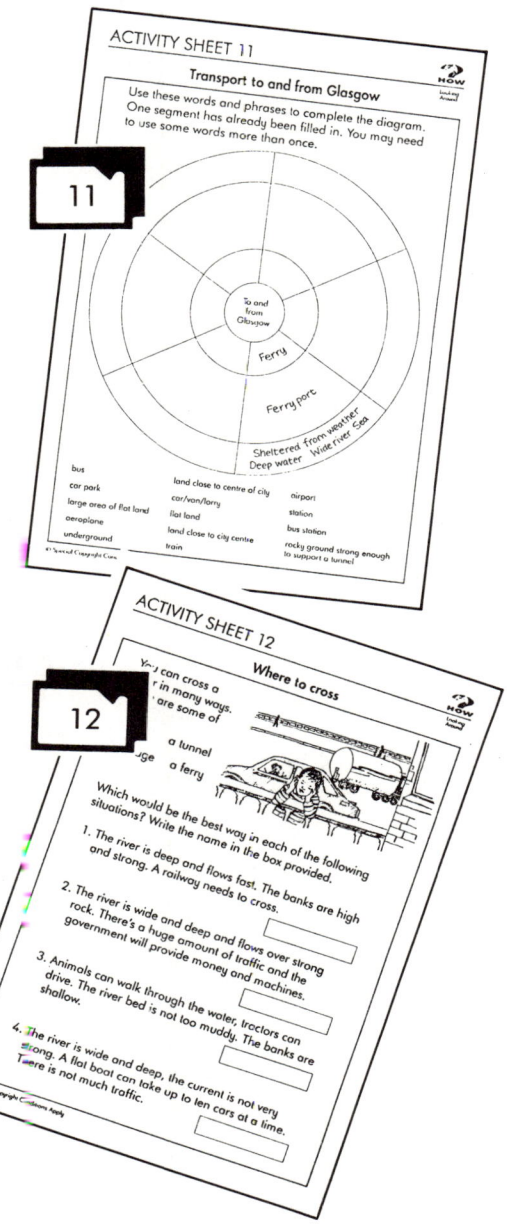

Evidence of attainment	*Bases of assessment*
Child uses geographical vocabulary in talking about the city	Oral
Child recognizes and talks about the features in the photos	Oral
Child matches transport requirements to transport	Product

ACTIVITY 10: MAKING PLACES

Learning Opportunities

There are opportunities for children to develop the understanding, skills and attitudes involved in:

▲ looking at the different sizes of settlements that are found in the United Kingdom

▲ looking at the structure of settlements

▲ investigating the different uses of buildings in settlements

Background Information

In this activity the geographical skill being developed is the ability to discuss a familiar place using geographical vocabulary. Settlements can be investigated via pictures, maps and photographs as well as through direct discussion with the children about the place where they live. The Attainment Target specifically directs this activity at level 1 to talking, and the useful interchange of ideas that this can generate in small groups is something to be encouraged in all the activities. At level 2 geographical vocabulary and the use of photographs and pictures is suggested in order that the children (with assistance if needed) can pick out familiar features from their local area and also from the photographs in the book. Wherever they live they will be able to compare their settlement with a larger or smaller one from their textbook. Why settlements are located where they are and why they have developed in the way that they have is of key interest for geographers. The latter point links across with history. Some functions of some settlements are contained in the name (e.g., market town, commuter village, tourist village) but as the size increases functions become uniform, and most cities have a common supply of shops, goods and services. If there is a specific function for some it is as a capital city. The naming of functions is of direct interest to human geographers who study the decisions that people make and the structures that these generate as settlements.

Teaching and Learning Notes

The activity is presented as a recipe because – put very simply – all settlements have the same basic ingredients with a few added extras to bulk up the size. The common denominator is houses or homes. These appear in all the settlements (even in the isolated farmhouse example), but as the size increases more types of buildings are found to satisfy the needs of the population. The Village Pie has the essential ingredients of a village, although there are villages where some of these may be missing. Henryd, for example, has a village shop which only opens once a week, and there is no pub. In some villages the school has also closed – often under protest, for the village loses a social as well as an educational centre. If you live in a village does your recipe differ? Point out to the children that although the farm is away from the road, the houses are at

---

Assessment opportunities

KEY SoA: Gg4/2a

Statement of Attainment

Demonstrate an understanding that most homes are part of a settlement, and that settlements vary in size

either edge of it. Houses were built so close to the road originally for easy access. Later this allowed houses to be connected to water, electric and gas mains.

With an increase of size the town 'roast' contains a greater variety of buildings, most notably shopping and transport centres and a building where people who control housing/business development, transport and schools work. The increase in settlement size means that there are people whose job is to decide how the town should be run: there is a plan which unfolds as the town is 'built' by the children. The houses are away from the factories and are found in small units together, often near a shopping centre.

This is true of the city which can appear to be a number of towns stuck together: the factories occur in groups and the centre of the city usually has buildings and offices where people work. New houses tend to be located more towards the outside of the city near the main roads so that people can easily drive to the centre. Notice different sized roads, and the fact that people can fairly easily catch a bus or train – railways are not a ready form of transport for people who live in the countryside. There are also blocks of flats because there is less space for building houses, so this is a more economical use of land.

Extensions and Variations

Children could extend the work done in the pupil book by making the recipes three dimensional. Mathematical counting apparatus, such as Unifix, Multilink cubes etc. could be used to make houses, shops, factories, schools and other buildings. Different colours could be used for the different types of buildings. The children could then construct a settlement using the maps in the textbook as guides or they can invent their own pattern. It will be apparent if they have grasped the difference not only in size, but also in function with the inclusion of different buildings. They should be encouraged to produce a key for the buildings as this will provide an introduction to the idea of keys which will be looked at in detail in Gg1/4f. It is often easier to see what is happening when a model is used instead of a map or picture. If the pupils create a model of a village, then they could make a map of it and this would provide an extension of Gg1/3c. There are links to Mathematics and Technology in fulfilling this activity.

Evidence of attainment

Child produces a settlement of the correct structure for the recipe being followed

Basis of assessment

Product

ACTIVITY 11: PUTTING PLACES IN THEIR PLACE

Learning Opportunities

There are opportunities for children to develop the understanding, skills and attitudes involved in:

▲ looking at simple small scale maps and identifying features on them
▲ locating their local area on the small scale map
▲ using atlases to find information about places

Background Information

The basic source of data for geographers is the map. These are produced at a variety of scales, from large scale, detailed maps of local areas to the small scale maps of parts of or whole countries. Small scale maps provide a view not dissimilar to a satellite photograph, but with colour and symbols used to clarify the information contained on it. Such maps are most useful for showing the position of cities, towns and villages in a country. They also show large physical features such as rivers and mountains or high ground. Major roads and railways are also shown, so that the connection between the towns is recorded. Sometimes physical features form the boundaries between countries and the border separating the two is a river or mountain range. Nearer to home, parish and county boundaries are also drawn along the line of physical features. The national curriculum states that pupils should have a knowledge of places – at level 2, this involves straightforward recognition of countries and the location of major cities and physical features. The pupils will already have experienced a sketch map (part of Iona) and will have drawn a route map. Now is a good time to explain that different maps exist for different purposes: street maps for finding your way, maps of main road networks for drivers, maps of physical features, of which the most common is the 1:50000 scale Ordnance Survey map. The OS maps contain all the features of a particular area, and are produced from aerial photographs all taken at the same time. The maps are then plotted by computer using standard symbols and colours. This is also a good time to show the location of the UK on a globe and/or map of the world and to introduce the idea of international relationships of scale and location.

Assessment opportunities	*Statements of Attainment*
KEY SoA: Gg2/2a	Name the countries of the United Kingdom
Other SoAs which could be assessed:	
Gg2/3a	Name the features on Maps A and C at the end of the programmes of study*
Gg2/3b	Demonstrate that they know the location of their local area within the country in which they live

Teaching and Learning Notes

Looking at the map of the United Kingdom will enable children to recognize the outline of the British Isles as a whole. What will probably not be familiar is the outline of the component countries on their own. This exercise is intended to make them look more closely at the map to find the detail that they will require to complete this task successfully.

The boundaries of the individual countries are not very clear on Map A in the National Curriculum document but by looking at the maps of each country and picking up the cues of rivers and capital cities the children should be able to familiarize themselves with the necessary detail quickly.

Help the children locate their own home towns on the map of the United Kingdom (Gg1/1e; Gg3/3b). Places mentioned in the book have been labelled as well, so that children can relate them to the places they know.

Extensions and Variations

Activity Sheet 13: *Map of the United Kingdom* shows a series of symbols: triangle = mountain ranges; circle = towns and cities; squares = rivers. The children have to identify the feature at the location of these symbols and name it. The places are mentioned in the pupil book. The children will need to use an atlas to identify the mountains and rivers. This will reinforce Gg 1/1d, 2/2a and provide an introduction to 3/3a and 3/3b. It will also familiarize them with the use of reference materials. The teacher will need to provide guidance and the children should work in groups.

13

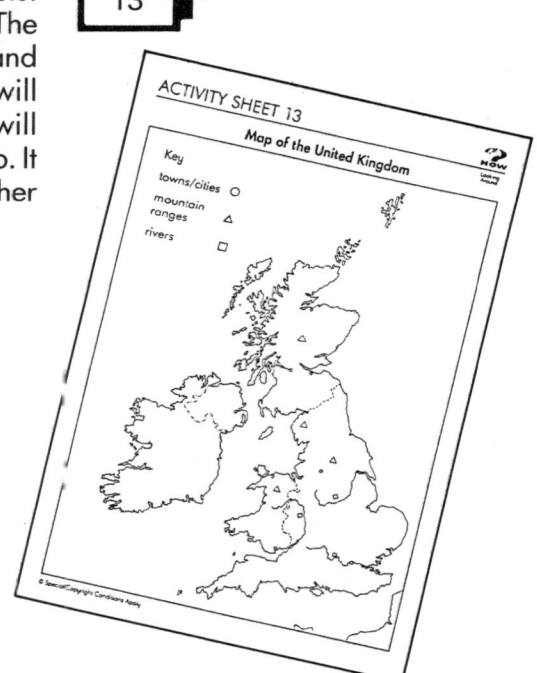

Evidence of attainment	*Bases of assessment*
Child names and locates the countries of the United Kingdom on a map	Oral
Child indicates her/his local area on a map of the United Kingdom	Observation/Oral
Child names the features on Map A in the National Curriculum document	Product

ACTIVITY 12: THE PLACE OF CHANGE

Learning Opportunities

There are opportunities for children to develop the understanding, skills and attitudes involved in:

▲ looking at ways of improving an environment

▲ discussing likes or dislikes about a place

▲ making plans for changing what they like or dislike about a place

Background Information

Environmental concerns have been made explicit within the geography curriculum, but also appear in the science curriculum in the themes used to explore scientific topics. As a result of media coverage children are frequently more aware of, and have better defined views on, environmental problems than many adults. The emphasis of Gg5/2c is placed on improving children's environments and this will obviously vary from area to area across the country. At a local level environmental problems are usually related to things which directly affect the individual, like litter, dog mess, pollution of local streams, noise from the neighbouring transport system. These will be fairly common to all areas. There may be specific activities locally which have damaged the environment and discussing these in groups will encourage the exchange of ideas. The economic status of an area inevitably affects the quality of the environment, a point which is made in the pupil book in the context of the decline of ports on the western side of the country. A strong feeling of community can reveal itself as pride in the environment, which may well be better cared for as a result. In areas where people do not mix, they may not acknowledge any responsibility to look after their environment.

Teaching and Learning Notes

1 Ugly places

After discussing likes and dislikes about their local area the children are encouraged to make a drawing from memory of how they think the place they dislike looks. It can be helpful if during the discussion they refer to the pictures in their book to see what they like and dislike about Cardiff and Belfast.

Assessment opportunities

KEY SoA: Gg5/2c

Other SoA which could be assessed:

Gg5/3b

Statements of Attainment

Suggest how they could improve the quality of their own environment

Describe an activity designed to improve the local environment or a place they have visited

2 Room for improvement

Here the children make a list of the features they have represented in their pictures which they feel are negative in the environment.

3 The new look

They can then allow their imagination to work on the features that they think are important for a good environment. Again refer to the improvements that have taken place in Belfast and Cardiff to initiate discussion.

Extensions and Variations

Activity Sheet 14: *Changing places* requires individual children to respond to a series of questions about ways in which environmental improvements can take place. These questions appear on the left of the page in a series of speech bubbles. Children write their responses next to the blank speech bubbles opposite. They choose the place and record its name at the top of the sheet.

Activity Sheet 15: *What would you add?* is a drawing of an old-fashioned school building, with a series of objects around it which might be added to improve the environment of the school. The activity draws on the children's own experience and provides a stimulus for ideas. The children should be encouraged to think up ideas that involve different senses (those are windchimes!) as well as opportunities for more varied play and a greener environment. Of course, some may already be familiar from their own school. There are links with Technology and Science. Encourage the children to justify their choice of objects, and explain why others were not chosen. This then reinforces Gg5/1b and translates it into a practical activity.

Evidence of attainment	Bases of assessment
Child talks about features which damage the local environment	Oral
Child selects objects and activities which would improve the local environment	Product/Oral

ACTIVITY 13: THE PLACE OF WATER

Learning Opportunities

There are opportunities for children to develop the understanding, skills and attitudes involved in:

▲ looking at the various types of water bodies on the surface of the earth

▲ studying the different uses people make of water

▲ considering the importance of water in people's lives

Background Information

In the pupil book the photographs show four different forms of water – namely a stream, a river (same thing, only bigger), a lake, and the sea (another change of scale and of composition too, as salt has been added). Bring out the way different forms are used for different purposes – the water at Bourton is useless for ships to sail up, but it may a pleasanter place for a picnic than a large river. Larger bodies of water are commonly used for recreational activities like boating and fishing. Indeed the use of water for leisure activities is growing. Seafishing is their livelihood for many people living in towns on the coast, both catching fish themselves and taking other people on trips to catch fish.

To sum up: water for drinking is essential for life; water provides an economic resource through fishing; it is used in power generation for driving or cooling turbines. People also use the sea to get rid of waste materials from towns and cities. Is there a stream or river near you, whose use compares with the examples shown here?

Water is the essence of the hydrological cycle which begins as rainfall, and moves to the sea in a sequence of channels. Ponds near the source of the river, lakes or reservoirs along its course, are areas where the water is stored. The hydrological cycle is touched on in *Where you Live* though its detailed study is a level 6 activity. Here we concentrate on the forms that liquid water takes on the ground. Its solid and gaseous forms are considered in the following chapters.

Assessment opportunities

KEY SoA: Gg3/2b

Statements of Attainment

Identify forms in which water occurs in the environment

Other SoA which could be assessed:

Gg3/3b

Describe what happens to rainwater when it hits the ground

Teaching and Learning Notes

1 Water names

The characteristics of streams, rivers, lakes and the sea are worked out through studying photographs. Differences can be blurred. It is not always easy to say just when a stream becomes a river, or when a river becomes a lake.

In this country coastal views are easy to find. The classifying of stretches of water is complicated by the range of local names. Lakes or ponds are variously known as broads, flashes, pools. What are the local names in your area?

2 Using water for fun

Water-based leisure activities are numerous and increasing all the time. Traditionally there are sports such as fishing, swimming, sailing, canoeing and rowing. More recently these have been joined by scubadiving, sailboarding (or windsurfing), and powerboat-related sports such as jetskiing, waterskiing and parascending. The list is large and local leisure centres will show what is available in your area.

Extensions and Variations

Activity Sheet 16: *Water in the environment* is a board game played with dice and counters which addresses Gg3/3b, Gg3/2b and reinforces Gg3/1a (recognizing that water is part of the environment). The source of the river is shown at the top of the board and the river starts to flow after heavy rain; this provides a brief introduction to some of the vocabulary used at level 4 describing river systems. As the river flows towards the sea different forms and features are encountered such as a waterfall, reservoir, estuary, along with such watery events as a flood. Several discussion points can be picked up, for example what happens to a river after several very dry summers, the impact of a flood, and the effect of tides. Links with History and Science can be made here and there is potential for creative writing from the point of view of the river.

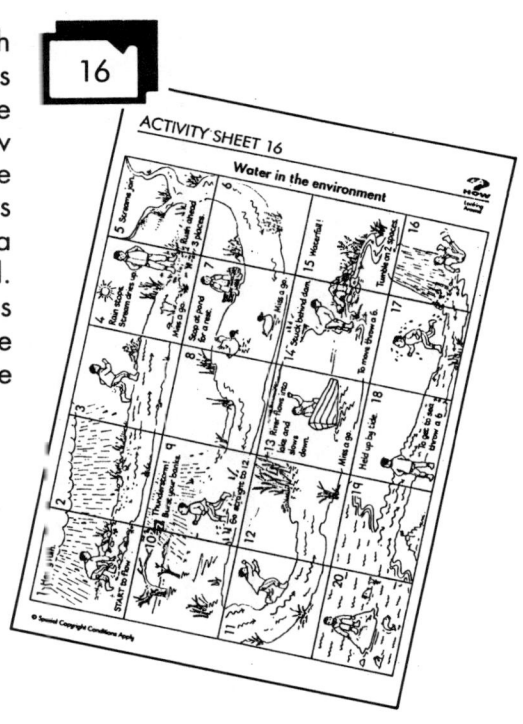

Evidence of attainment	Bases of assessment
Child writes a sentence naming several water sports which take place beside, on or in the water	Product
Child uses vocabulary describing water in the environment when playing the board game	Oral/Observation

ACTIVITY 14: CHANGING SEASONS: WINTER

Learning Opportunities

There are opportunities for children to develop the understanding, skills and attitudes involved in:

▲ observing that the weather changes through the year
▲ recognizing the various forms in which water occurs in the environment
▲ describing what happens to water at the earth's surface

Background Information

The year is divided into four broad time periods called the seasons: the different weather associated with the seasons is controlled by the Earth's movement around the sun. The Earth is tilted on its axis and in winter when the northern hemisphere is tilted away from the sun the days are short and the nights long because the sun is low in the sky. When the northern hemisphere tilts towards the sun the days are long, the nights short and it is summer; in between these extremes are spring and autumn. The Earth's distance from the sun should mean that it is a cold planet, but because of an envelope of 'greenhouse gases' (carbon dioxide and a trace of some others) most of the heat reaching the surface is trapped in the lower layers of the atmosphere. One of the most important features of the atmosphere is the presence of water vapour as clouds which prevent much of the sun's heat (25%) from reaching the surface. Another 25% is blocked out by dust, water vapour or reflected from bright surfaces such as snow. There is therefore a complex and delicate balance between heat input and output, which means that there are different weather patterns within seasons as well as between them which are not easy to predict. This point should be emphasized to the children: there is often very wet weather in the summer – August can bring heavy storms – and there can be very mild and sunny weather in the autumn or spring. Winter will mean different things to people in different parts of the country: in Scotland and in Kent it snows quite heavily in winter, but in Cheshire hardly ever. It also snows more often and is colder in the upland areas of the United Kingdom.

Assessment opportunities	*Statements of Attainment*
KEY SoAs: Gg3/2a	Recognize seasonal weather patterns
Gg3/2b	Identify the forms in which water appears in the environment
Other SoA which could be assessed:	
Gg3/3b	Describe what happens to rainwater when it reaches the ground

Teaching and Learning Notes

1 Dressing the part

In winter it is cold and if the wind blows as well then it feels *much* colder: this is called the wind chill factor. It is important to keep warm especially if the wind is blowing. Clothing should be chosen to provide layers that trap air to provide insulation. The Inuit dress in furs where the hairs trap a layer of air which keeps out the Arctic cold. The poem reminds us that, although it can be enjoyable, the wind can also be strong enough to blow smaller people over.

2 Poem

All the seasons have their evocative features, and in this activity the children think about what winter means to them. Encourage them to use all their senses. Smells provide vivid cues to memory, and so do sound and touch. Remind them of the the feel of ice and snow. Use the poem and the photographs as a basis for discussing the things which make winter.

Extensions and Variations

Activity Sheets 17–20 relate to all the seasons. The Activity Sheets should be cut into cards which the children can use to play pelmanism or games where they collect sets or pairs of cards. The purpose of the activity is to underline the physical, weather and human conditions associated with the seasons (Gg3/2a). It will familiarize the children with the type of weather peculiar to the United Kingdom, and provide a basis for comparison with weather in other parts of the world (Gg3/3a). It also allows the development of recognition skills and association of features with weather.

   The tree chosen to illustrate the Tree cards is the elder, whose creamy flowers and black-currant coloured berries will be familiar to town and country children alike.

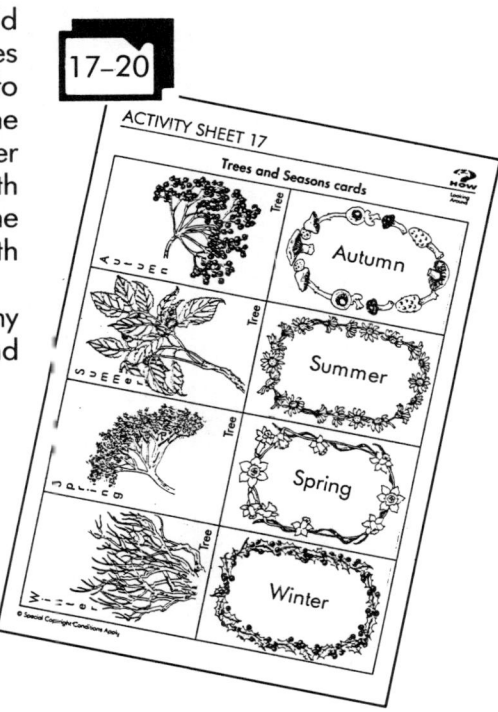

17–20

Evidence of attainment	Bases of assessment
Child lists the clothes which are necessary to keep warm in winter	Product
Child describes to a partner the type of weather found in their favourite season	Oral
Child knows that snow is a form of water that occurs when the weather is cold	Product/Oral

ACTIVITY 15: CHANGING SEASONS: SPRING

Learning Opportunities

There are opportunities for children to develop the understanding, skills and attitudes involved in:

▲ looking at different types of weather

▲ investigating the different forms of water in the environment

▲ studying what happens to water when it reaches the ground

Background Information

In spring the sun is still low above the horizon and the sun's rays have to travel through a greater thickness of atmosphere as a result. This means that it can be bright and warm but it does not become really hot. The day length increases very quickly and the combination of more daylight and warmer temperatures promotes rapid growth in plants. Buds appear on deciduous trees, and bulbs and shoots push out of the ground. This may be dangerous for the plant if the growth is too early and there is then a late frost. There have been several years during the last decade when there has been frost and snow at the start of the cricket season in May. If the weather is unseasonably mild, plants start growing too soon, and this makes them susceptible to damage. It is important for the plants to produce leaves quickly however so that they can trap the energy from the sun's rays to make the sugars which they need to grow. Water is evaporated from the seas and lakes on the Earth's surface and rises into the atmosphere where it moves around, sometimes as clouds before falling down as heavy showers. More evaporation means more rainfall because the hydrological cycle maintains a balance between its parts. The cold air of winter cannot evaporate as much water from the earth's surface, as the sun's energy in spring can, but with so much water going up there are heavier showers when it comes down. The newspapers and weather reports on radio or television give a good idea about the temperatures rising and the days lengthening: if these are recorded for three or four weeks (just the same night every week would do) and then plotted they would show these changes clearly.

Assessment opportunities	Statements of Attainment
KEY SoAs: Gg3/2a	Recognize seasonal weather patterns
Gg3/2b	Identify the forms in which water occurs in the environment
Other SoA which could be assessed:	
Gg3/3b	Describe what happens to rainwater when it reaches the ground

Teaching and Learning Notes

1 Spring flowers

There are a large number of plants flowering in spring and this activity provides the chance to identify them with the help of reference books. The Scarlet Pimpernel and the Horse Chestnut are two that the children could look out for in particular. There are good links with Science here in terms of growing things.

2 Weather words

This is an activity in which the children think of words associated with spring weather. The activity is reinforced by using the spring flowers as a design for the border surrounding the words. The children can use their own flowers if they wish, but they must be spring flowers.

The poem 'And Suddenly Spring' evokes the changeable weather of spring and should stimulate ideas. It draws attention to spring's effect on trees (linking up with the spread on wind on pages 42–3) and the way spring rain can catch people out when they least expect it!

Extensions and Variations

Activity Sheets 17–20 relate to all the seasons. The Activity Sheets should be cut into cards which the children can use to play pelmanism or games where they collect sets or pairs of cards. The purpose of the activity is to underline the physical, weather and human conditions associated with the seasons (Gg3/2a). It will familiarize the children with the type of weather peculiar to the United Kingdom, and provide a basis for comparison with weather in other parts of the world (Gg3/3a). It also allows the development of recognition skills and association of features with weather.

Evidence of attainment	Bases of assessment
Child writes words which describe water in the spring	Product
Child identifies flowers which are related to spring and draws them in a pattern	Product/Oral
Child talks about rainwater when it reaches the ground	Oral

ACTIVITY 16: CHANGING SEASONS: SUMMER

Learning Opportunities

There are opportunities for children to develop the understanding, skills and attitudes involved in:

▲ looking at different types of weather
▲ investigating the different forms of water in the environment
▲ studying what happens to water when it reaches the ground

Background Information

During the summer the northern half of the earth is tilted closest to the sun and this is therefore the hottest time of the year in the United Kingdom. Food for plant growth is created by energy from the sun and water containing minerals and nutrients from the soil. The chemical reaction which causes this conversion is called photosynthesis. The summer is when trees and plants grow fastest – think of how often lawns have to be mowed at different times of the year. In the summer the rate of growth is affected not just by the sun's energy but also by how much water there is in the soil. If there is a drought (as there was in 1976 and for some years in the late 1980s) then a tree may lose its leaves early in order to survive. Some plants may die because of the lack of water. You can test how quickly water is evaporated (turned to a vapour) by putting a saucer of water in direct sunlight and another with the same amount of water in the shade and recording how quickly they dry up. Trees use huge amounts of water, hundreds of litres a day, and act like large pumps taking the water out of the soil and releasing it as a vapour into the atmosphere. If you tie a clear plastic bag over some leaves on the end of a branch the water being released will be trapped in the bag and you can record the amount that is being lost through only a few leaves. If a leaf is cut from a plant and its stem immediately placed in dyed water then the way the water moves can be seen as it colours the veins it moves through. Summer days are very much longer. In the north of Scotland it is possible to read a newspaper by the light of the sun after midnight. As a result, some animals such as bats which would not normally be seen because they come out after dark can be observed in the evenings.

Assessment opportunities	Statements of Attainment
KEY SoAs: Gg3/2a	Recognize seasonal weather patterns
Gg3/2b	Identify the forms in which water occurs in the environment
Other SoA which could be assessed	
Gg3/3b	Describe what happens to rainwater when it reaches the ground

Teaching and Learning Notes

1 Tangletalk

A border is used again to highlight the feel of summer; the colours now are bright and and more varied than in spring which is dominated by the green of new leaves. The task of rewriting the poem encourages the children to identify the words which are 'not summer' and then to replace them with appropriate ones of their choice. The picture of a summer's day and the small poem are there to provide a selection of prompts.

2 A summer's day

This activity focuses on the sights, sounds, smells, tastes and feeling of a summer's day which are conveyed by the picture. Encourage the children to use all their senses when discussing what happens in the day. Some of the words used in the poems may help in the activity. The children can choose whether to tell the story in the first or third person.

Extensions and Variations

Activity Sheets 17–20 relate to all the seasons. The Activity Sheets should be cut into cards which the children can use to play pelmanism or games where they collect sets or pairs of cards. The purpose of the activity is to underline the physical, weather and human conditions associated with the seasons (Gg3/2a). It will familiarize the children with the type of weather peculiar to the United Kingdom, and provide a basis for comparison with weather in other parts of the world (Gg3/3a). It also allows the development of recognition skills and association of features with weather.

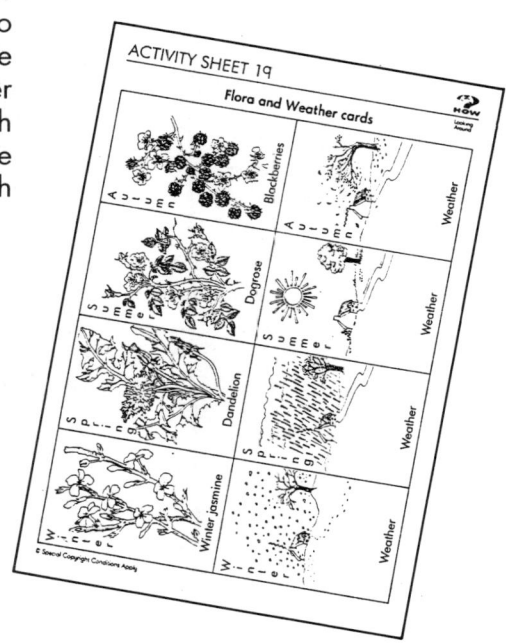

Evidence of attainment	Bases of assessment
Child recognizes and writes in context words representing summer	Product
Child discusses what the weather is like during a summer day	Oral
Child describes some of the effects of summer weather on plants and animals	Oral

ACTIVITY 17: CHANGING SEASONS: AUTUMN

Learning Opportunities

There are opportunities for children to develop the understanding, skills and attitudes involved in:

▲ looking at different types of weather
▲ investigating the different forms of water in the environment
▲ studying what happens to water when it reaches the ground

Background Information

In the environment there are **cycles** of material and **flows** of energy. In autumn the cycle of growth that happened in spring and summer is replaced by a cycle of decay and replenishment of nutrient stores from the dying plant and animal life. This is natural **recycling**. Less energy reaches the Earth from the sun (because of the tilt effect), the days start to shorten and colder weather becomes more frequent. At this time of year water can be seen in other forms, as fog and dew. The dew found on the ground in the early morning is formed by condensation of water vapour from the colder air at night. This happens in late summer as well after warm days. Dew is formed by the same process as the condensation you can observe when your breath falls on a cold surface like glass or metal. During the autumn the weather is very changeable and often there are storms with strong winds and rain. The British Isles lie in the path of depressions moving in from the west. These are rain bearing, slowly spinning belts of cloud which travel across the country particularly in the autumn and winter, although they can occur at any season. Part of the cycle of decay involves mushrooms and toadstools which live on dead plant material and they can be seen most often in September and October. Sometimes they grow in circles called 'Fairy Rings'. Deciduous trees lose their leaves which rot down to return nutrients to their roots. Seeds and nuts also fall and are moved around by animals, wind and water to begin the cycle of growth again in the spring.

Assessment opportunities *Statements of Attainment*

KEY SoAs: Gg3/2a Recognize seasonal weather patterns

Gg3/2b Identify the forms in which water occurs in the environment

Other SoA which could be assessed:

Gg3/3b Describe what happens to rainwater when it reaches the ground

Teaching and Learning Notes

1 Autumn weekend

One way of focusing on the main characteristics of autumn weather is to consider the types of clothes most suitable for this season. This links with the word search at the start of the book, which suggests that food and warmth are necessary for survival. Encourage the children to say from their own experience whether warmth or waterproofs are more important. There are obvious links to Technology if the backpack has to last a weekend and still be portable! Photos C and D will provide clues and focus discussion and children should be encouraged to think of fog and dew, with perhaps a touch of frost freezing the dew, as further ways in which water could affect them.

2 Season's choice

Replies will be purely subjective but children will be able to identify the characteristics of the seasons and the linked festivals (e.g. bonfire night) which make them their favourites. What they must do is to explain what the weather is like in the season they choose, thus reinforcing the link between weather and season. Variations within seasons seem to have increased in the last twenty years, but broadly speaking the weather 'type' for a season still holds good.

Extensions and Variations

Activity Sheets 17–20 relate to all the seasons. The Activity Sheets should be cut into cards which the children can use to play pelmanism or games where they collect sets or pairs of cards. The purpose of the activity is to underline the physical, weather and human conditions associated with the seasons (Gg3/2a). It will familiarize the children with the type of weather peculiar to the United Kingdom, and provide a basis for comparison with weather in other parts of the world (Gg3/3a). It also allows the development of recognition skills and association of features with weather.

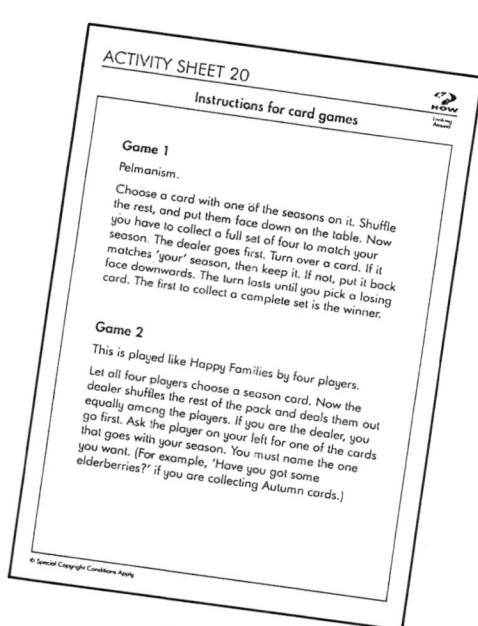

ACTIVITY SHEET 20

Instructions for card games

Game 1

Pelmanism.

Choose a card with one of the seasons on it. Shuffle the rest, and put them face down on the table. Now you have to collect a full set of four to match your season. The dealer goes first. Turn over a card. If it matches 'your' season, then keep it. If not, put it back face downwards. The turn lasts until you pick a losing card. The first to collect a complete set is the winner.

Game 2

This is played like Happy Families by four players.

Let all four players choose a season card. Now the dealer shuffles the rest of the pack and deals them out equally among the players. If you are the dealer, you go first. Ask the player on your left for one of the cards that goes with your season. You must name the one you want. (For example, 'Have you got some elderberries?' if you are collecting Autumn cards.)

© Special Copyright Conditions Apply

Evidence of attainment	Bases of assessment
Child produces an appropriate list of clothing for the seasonal weather	Product
Child identifies a season and accurately describes the weather associated with it	Oral
Child talks about the different forms in which water occurs during the season chosen	Oral

ACTIVITY 18: MEASURING THE WEATHER

Learning Opportunities

There are opportunities for children to develop the understanding, skills and attitudes involved in:

▲ making a record of weather over a period of time
▲ investigating the factors which affect temperature locally
▲ looking at weather changes in a seasonal framework

Background Information

One of the most obvious features of weather, commented upon by millions of people every day, is the temperature. The heat from the sun is the power which keeps Earth's atmosphere circulating. It raises the temperature at different places on the Earth's surface which in turn warm the air above them. The hot air rises and cool air moves in to take its place. The degree of heating depends on the angle at which the rays strike the surface: the higher the sun is in the sky the hotter its rays because they are spread over a smaller area. When the sun is low above the horizon the rays are more widely spread and heat the surface more feebly. The sun is at its highest for the United Kingdom during the summer which is why days are hotter; in winter the sun is low and its heating power is limited, particularly when there is a lot of water vapour in the air.

Temperature is therefore controlled directly by sunlight, although if the air's moisture content is high (increased humidity), summer days can be uncomfortably warm, even when the sun is behind clouds. Once again weather proves to be more complex than it seems at first. Describing the seasonal differences in temperature is a level 5 activity (3/5a), but Spread 18 provides a basic introduction to the underlying ideas. Temperature is measured by a thermometer. Maximum and minimum combination thermometers which record the highest and lowest temperature of a day, week, month or year can yield interesting data. Recording the temperature at hourly intervals during the day can be a rewarding exercise. It provides figures which can be plotted as a graph or bar chart to show change on a small scale.

Teaching and Learning Notes

1 Fill in the gaps

The 'fill in the gap' exercise will quickly assess whether children know the correct vocabulary. These terms can be used to make a subjective record of the weather over a time period, e.g., a week. The children could then identify the hottest and coldest days of a week and place the other days in order of heat between the extremes.

Assessment opportunities
KEY SoA: Gg1/2d

Statement of Attainment
Record weather observations made over a short period

2 Complete the sentences

This is a simple completion activity which recalls information and reinforces the factual content of the syllabus.

3 Fun in the sun

Another simple activity, but one which requires a connection to be made between the weather and the activities which it allows. The physical conditions caused by the sun and the effect they have can be the subject of discussion: do they make some activities uncomfortable compared with others?

Extensions and Variations

Activity Sheet 21: *How a thermometer works* is designed to familiarize the child with the technology involved in recording the temperature. The temperature can be displayed in a variety of ways (e.g. digital readout from a probe) but the most common way is to observe the expansion of a confined thread of mercury in a tube coming from the reservoir at the bottom of the instrument. Mercury is the only pure metal which is found as a liquid at the Earth's surface, which means that when heated it always behaves in the same way, and does not have to change from a solid to a liquid. Consequently the scale at the side of the tube can be small without being difficult to read. This scale is divided into degrees Celsius, although on older instruments the scale was Fahrenheit (both named after scientists). People in this country are familiar with both scales (depending on their age), so weather forecasters give temperatures in both scales. There is scope to talk about science and the effects of heat upon substances: in this case the expansion of metal has been adapted by technology to provide a useful scale.

Knowing the temperature is useful for more than the record books: it allows us to see patterns and then predict what is likely to happen. It is also important from a health standpoint because very young and very old people are affected by very high and very low temperatures and need to be warmed or cooled accordingly.

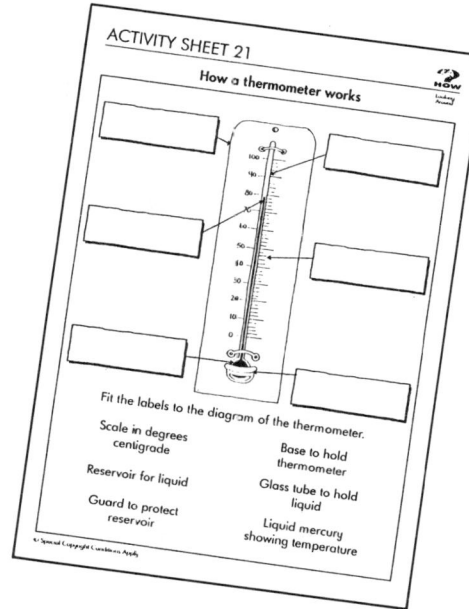

21

ACTIVITY SHEET 21
How a thermometer works

Fit the labels to the diagram of the thermometer.

Scale in degrees centigrade

Reservoir for liquid

Guard to protect reservoir

Base to hold thermometer

Glass tube to hold liquid

Liquid mercury showing temperature

Evidence of attainment

Child records comparative feelings of temperature appropriately in the table

Basis of assessment

Product

ACTIVITY 19: IT'S RAINING, IT'S POURING

Learning Opportunities

There are opportunities for children to develop the understanding, skills and attitudes involved in:

▲ looking at rainfall as part of the environment
▲ investigating the forms in which water occurs in the environment
▲ recognizing the seasonal variation in rainfall and other precipitation
▲ studying the forms of cloud in the atmosphere

Background Information

Rain falls as part of the hydrological cycle, in which water vapour held in the atmosphere condenses and falls to the earth to be channelled to the sea in rivers. Water vapour which is normally an invisible gas requires a nucleus (a small particle) to enable it to condense. This can be dust, smoke or salt crystals and for this reason rainfall will occur more often over cities where there are more of these condensation nuclei. If the air around a cloud is dry it may evaporate. At other times it will continue to grow, turning into a rain cloud as water vapour collects and saturates it.

The large lumpy clouds most often seen in the summer are called cumulus clouds. They have their own internal currents, allowing them to grow and carry more water which eventually falls as a heavy shower. Rain most frequently falls from clouds which are very dark to look at because they have so much water in them. The white clouds of summer are formed when the water vapour carried up by warm rising air condenses as the air cools. The mechanism behind this is as follows: warm air can hold more water vapour than cold air. But warm air rises, and as it rises it becomes colder. Warm, moist air, forced to rise as it reaches a mountain range, will grow cool, and rain will fall. Moist winds blowing from the west rise over the mountains which are found all down this side of the British Isles and as a result the western side of the UK is wetter than the east.

Clouds which are very high above the ground are made of ice crystals and look feathery or wispy.

Mist and fog are formed in a different way. At night in hilly areas the ground cools quickly and as a result the air immediately above it is cooled, making the water vapour in it condense and form a fog or mist. Because the air is cooled, it also becomes heavier and sinks down the hillsides into the valleys where it stays until the heat from the sun above evaporates it once more. Fog is a cloud which touches the ground.

Assessment opportunities	Statements of Attainment
KEY SoA: Gg3/2b	Identify the forms in which water occurs in the environment
Gg3/2a	Recognize seasonal weather patterns

Other SoA which could be assessed:

Gg3/3b	Describe what happens to rainwater when it reaches the ground

Teaching and Learning Notes

1 Describing how rain falls

You will have to provide some help with this activity in terms of background information; use the factual material provided above, but also encourage the children to use reference books. There is a link with English and Science and the children can be creative as well as being factual.

2 Observing the weather

This task is not as difficult as it might appear; the amount of cloud is measured in octas (eighths of cover), so that at 0 there is no cloud, at 4 half the sky is covered with cloud and at 8 the cloud cover is complete. This is a straightforward scale and can soon be grasped to make estimates. This exercise has links with Mathematics. Writing the sentence is an opportunity for the child's observation and imagination to combine.

3 Looking at clouds

This is straightforward observation, but the shape and type of cloud are important as they can be used as weather predictors. Once the children have drawn their clouds, they can try to recognize the type from reference material.

Extensions and Variations

Activity Sheet 22: *What goes up must come down* provides an introduction to the hydrological cycle which is the most important cycle in the environment as far as people are concerned. It is powered by solar energy and is also to a certain extent self cleaning, in the way it filters through soil and rocks as part of its movement. The details of the hydrological cycle are addressed at level 6 where an explanation is required of the components. It is useful however to look at the overall cycle in outline here as it will be picked up as a theme in *Where You Live*. The children will have to match the descriptions of the stages of the cycle to the diagram to familiarize themselves with the names used and the order in which they appear.

This cycle is basic to all geographical physical processes and provides a good link between physical, environmental and human geography. In fact, water is the common denominator in determining the majority of geographical activity. There are also links to Science and Technology.

Evidence of attainment	Bases of assessment
Child is aware that rainfall is part of a larger cycle of water	Oral
Child knows and can talk about the weather in the different seasons particularly the cloud and rain	Oral
Child labels the main elements of the hydrological cycle	Product

ACTIVITY 20: BLOW WIND BLOW

Learning Opportunities

There are opportunities for children to develop the understanding, skills and attitudes involved in:

▲ recognizing that wind is part of the natural environment
▲ investigating the change in wind characteristics during the seasons
▲ using a variety of methods for measuring the strength of the wind

Background Information

The atmosphere is in constant motion and its movement is powered by solar energy. Where the ground is warm and heats the air above it, the air rises and pulls surrounding air into the 'gap'. When it rises the air cools. It always rises at the equator and always sinks at the poles thus creating areas of low and high pressure. Winds flow from areas of high pressure to areas of low pressure because nature always attempts to achieve a balance. If there was not always incoming energy from the sun, highs and lows would be cancelled out and the atmosphere would not circulate. As a result there would be no seasons and no weather, and therefore not much for people to talk about! Fortunately, these differences do exist and the greater they are the stronger the winds that move between them. Winds distribute heat about the surface of the earth and transport seeds and tiny insects, as well as dust and pollutants. Winds vary from gentle breezes to strong hurricanes with wind speeds over 100 miles per hour. Where there are mountains winds can blow at speeds of nearly 200 miles per hour and there are few days of gentle breezes. In the British Isles strong winds blow mainly from the south-west, so Scotland and the west coast tend to be more windy than the rest of the country. The mountain ranges along the western side of the islands shelter the central and eastern areas from the strongest winds. Wind speed can be measured qualitatively (Beaufort Scale) or quantitatively using an anemometer. This is a set of three cups on a spindle which is rotated by the wind, recording an electrical impulse which is counted and shown on a digital display. In hand held instruments the windspeed drives the cups and thus the spindle: the rotation of the spindle moves a needle along a horizontal scale on the instrument's body. Instruments fixed to a high point on a building, like the one in the photograph, record the wind speed on instruments far below.

Teaching and Learning Notes

1 Using a weather vane

This is a straightforward question-and-answer exercise to ascertain whether the child understands what instruments are used to measure the wind. In the question of the weather vane, children may go on to consider the link between wind direction and weather type.

Assessment opportunities
KEY SoA: Gg3/2a

Statement of Attainment
Recognize seasonal weather patterns

2 The Beaufort Scale

In this activity children apply their understanding of the Beaufort scale from their tree example to the behaviour of other objects. They can demonstrate that other objects including buildings can be used to estimate wind speed. Later on you may wish to reinforce this activity using different exemplars.

Extensions and Variations

Weather vanes are one of the oldest objects used by forecasters and come in a wide range of designs, though traditionally they were cockerels. Winds from different directions bring different weather. From the north and east they may bring cold weather with frost, whilst from the south west they are more likely to bring warm, wet weather

Do the weather vanes in your local area come in special designs? You many wish to introduce Mathematics and Technology into their study. There are also links with Science and Art.

As an introduction to Gg3/4a it is useful to investigate how the wind behaves in the local area. This can involve a study around the school to decide which side is the windiest and which the most sheltered. One way of showing visually how the wind moves around a building is to puff talcum powder into the air and see which way it moves. This is particulary interesting near the edge of a wall where the wind swirls around. Record if the wind swirls up or down and if it moves faster near the building or further away; this can be done by moving out from the building in a straight line, puffing and recording. You can use this investigation to talk about what winds might do as they move around or over mountains. The same principles apply, but on a different scale.

Evidence of attainment

Child talks about how wind differs between the seasons

Basis of assessment

Oral

ACTIVITY 21: JUST FOR THE RECORD

Learning Opportunities

There are opportunities for the children to develop the understanding, skills and attitudes involved in:

▲ observing and recording changes of weather over a short time

▲ using a large scale map of the local area around the school to identify features

Background Information

Geography links with many other subjects, including Science, History, Mathematics, Art, Technology and English. There are many topical issues in local areas and these can be seen in relation to national and even international problems. By studying their local area the children develop investigative and other geographical skills which enable them to understand the character of places. The differences and similarities between settlements, the physical nature of places, the human decisions which create or halt development, the environmental control on people's activities and the way people affect the environment are all discovered initially by studying 'where you live'. Major variations in the geography of areas are primarily the result of differences of scale, and this is clearly seen in the function and development of settlements. Weather can be mild or severe; distance determines how people communicate; numbers of people determine the amount of transport, industry, and housing. All these are simple illustrations of a change of scale. Conflict and environmental damage may follow from attempts to change a place too quickly.

The geographer's interest in the causes and effects of change is reflected in Attainment Target 5 and the children will encounter this at levels 4–6 in the primary sector. To tackle the issues in human and physical geography (A.T. 2,3,4) the child needs to develop the skills required to analyse and interpret maps, photographs, pictures and secondary sources in an accurate and critical way. The material in this book should initiate this process and provide the basis for development in the books which follow.

Assessment opportunities	Statements of Attainment
KEY SoAs: Gg2/3c	Use correct geographical vocabulary to identify types of landscape features and activities with which they are familiar in the local area
Gg1/2d	Record weather observations made over short period

Other SoA which could be assessed:

Gg1/3b	Use a large scale map to locate their own position and features outside the classroom

Teaching and Learning Notes

1 Keeping a record

Making a record of the main features of a place is a good place to start finding out about its character. This will enable the children to compare their notes with information about other places mentioned in the book, and encourage them to look in more detail at the place where they live. Reinforces 1/1b and 2/1a.

2 Recording the weather

The weather diary, which uses comparative terms rather than absolute values to describe how the weather is behaving, is a different kind of record. This diary can be recorded at various times through the year thus encouraging comparison between the seasons, as well as within them. A chart is provided on Activity Sheet 23.

P.S. Follow-up to word search

This reinforcement activity provides the answers to the word search and then indicates the pages on which they can be found. Just as they passed unnoticed on the page, so all the factors which were initially identified as essential for life and comfort are usually taken for granted in the day to day running of our lives.

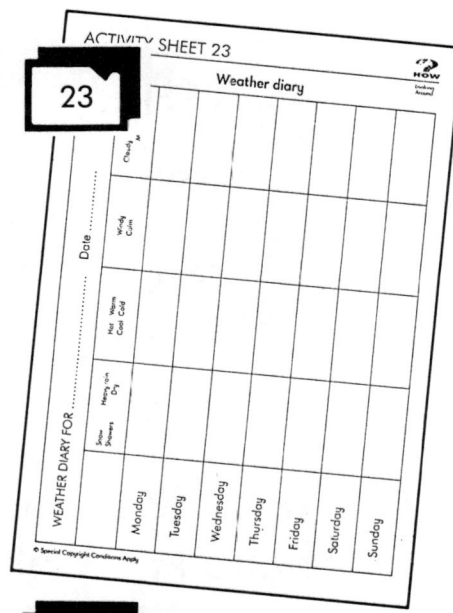

Extensions and Variations

All the activities in this book move the children from level 2 into level 3 by asking them to undertake activities which will give them a different view of the same issue or look at it in more depth. Some of the topics such as the hydrological cycle will not appear until level 6, but it is possible to make a basic introduction at this stage. Activity Sheet 24 is a variation of the record sheet. The child completes the sheet by filling in the boxes with a real and an invented weather symbol design. By designing their own weather symbol they need to consider how best to convey the message about the type of weather listed in the left hand column. This requires an understanding of the weather and allows the children to practise the geographer's skill of symbol design which is so important in maps to summarize information. Links are invited with Art and Science.

Evidence of attainment	Bases of assessment
Child accurately completes the record for My Place, using correct geographical vocabulary	Product
Child keeps a record of the weather for a week and can talk about what is recorded	Product/Oral
Child draws appropriate symbols for different weather	Product

ACTIVITY SHEET 1

Send a postcard

A postcard ready to send.

Add pictures to make a place you know about.

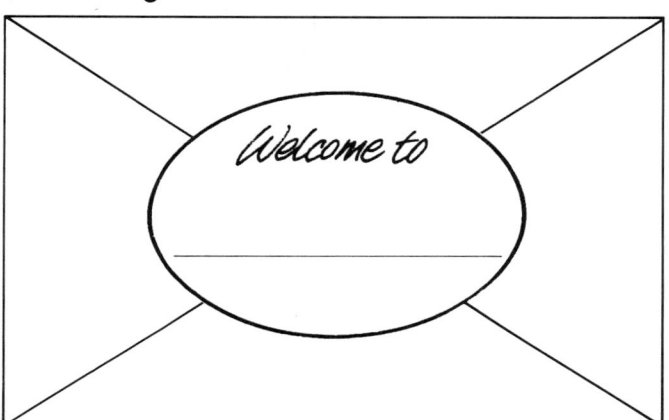

Write your own name and address here. Add a message.

Add pictures to make the place you live.

Write your teacher's name and school address here. Add a message.

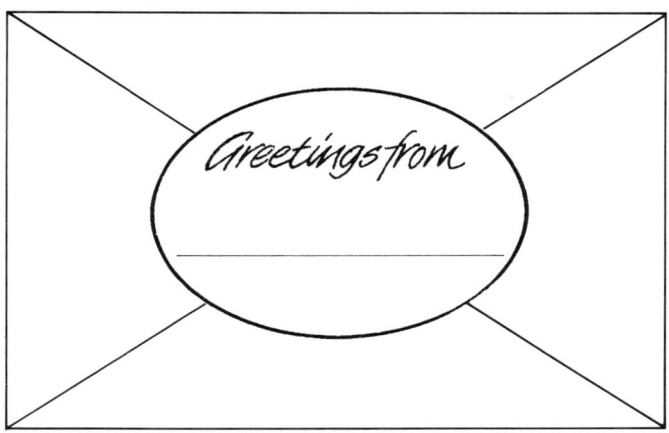

Sketch map of northern Iona

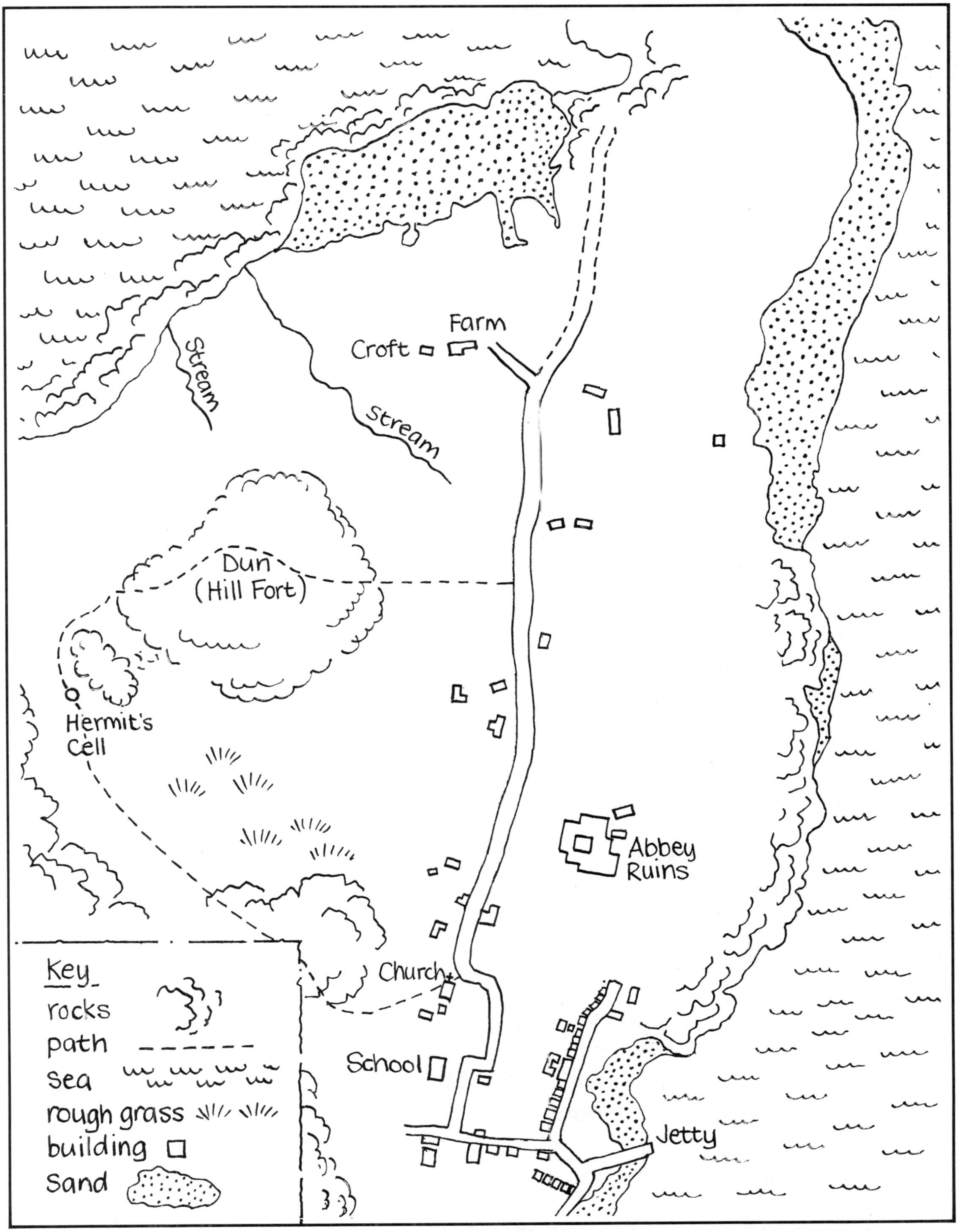

Stream

Stream

Croft ▫ ▭ Farm

Dun
(Hill Fort)

Hermit's
Cell

Abbey
Ruins

Church

School ▫

Jetty

Key
rocks
path - - -
sea
rough grass
building ▫
Sand

HOW
Looking
Around

Comparing Iona with near my school

	NEAR MY SCHOOL	NOT NEAR MY SCHOOL
IN IONA		
NOT IN IONA		

houses	farm	seashore
forest	railway station	lighthouse
swimming pool	jetty	abbey ruins
cinema	motorway	castle

To compare your place and Iona, you have to put the features on the list into the squares in the grid. This is how you do it.

1. Decide where each item is to be found.
2. If it is IN IONA it goes in one of the top two squares.
3. If it is NOT IN IONA it goes in one of the bottom two squares.
4. If it is NEAR YOUR SCHOOL it goes in one of the squares on the left hand side of the grid.
5. If it is NOT NEAR YOUR SCHOOL, it goes in one of the squares on the right hand side of the grid.

(So, if there is a cinema near you, it will go on the bottom left hand square, as there is no cinema in Iona. If there is a farm near you it will go in the top left hand square, because the map shows you that there is a farm in Iona as well.)

All the information about Iona can be found on the sketch map.

Looking
Around

My special place

To remember my special place
where I love to go I keep…

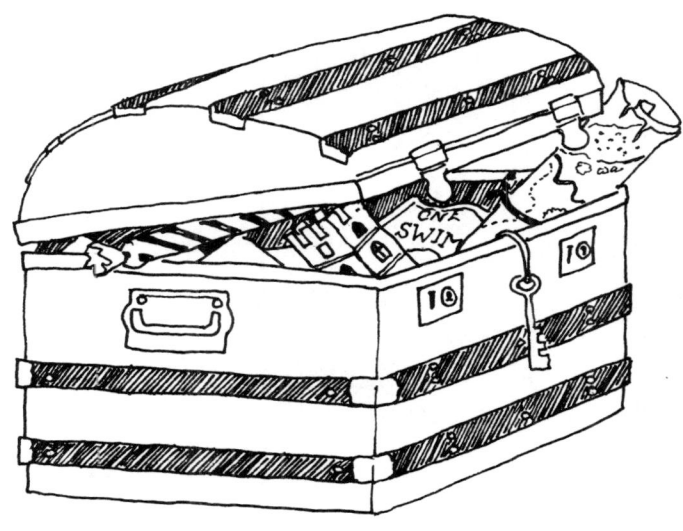

To remember my special place
where I love to go I keep…

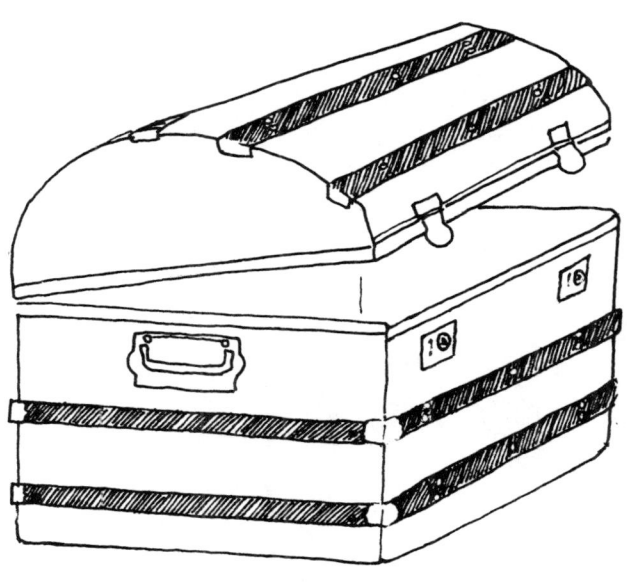

Looking
Around

Things to see in Henryd, Wales

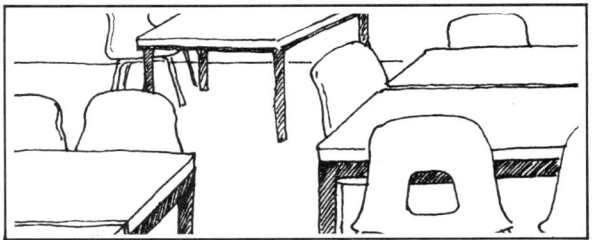

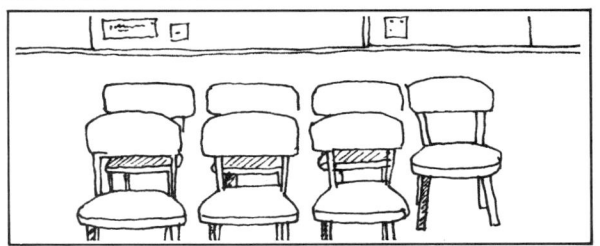

ACTIVITY SHEET 6

On the way

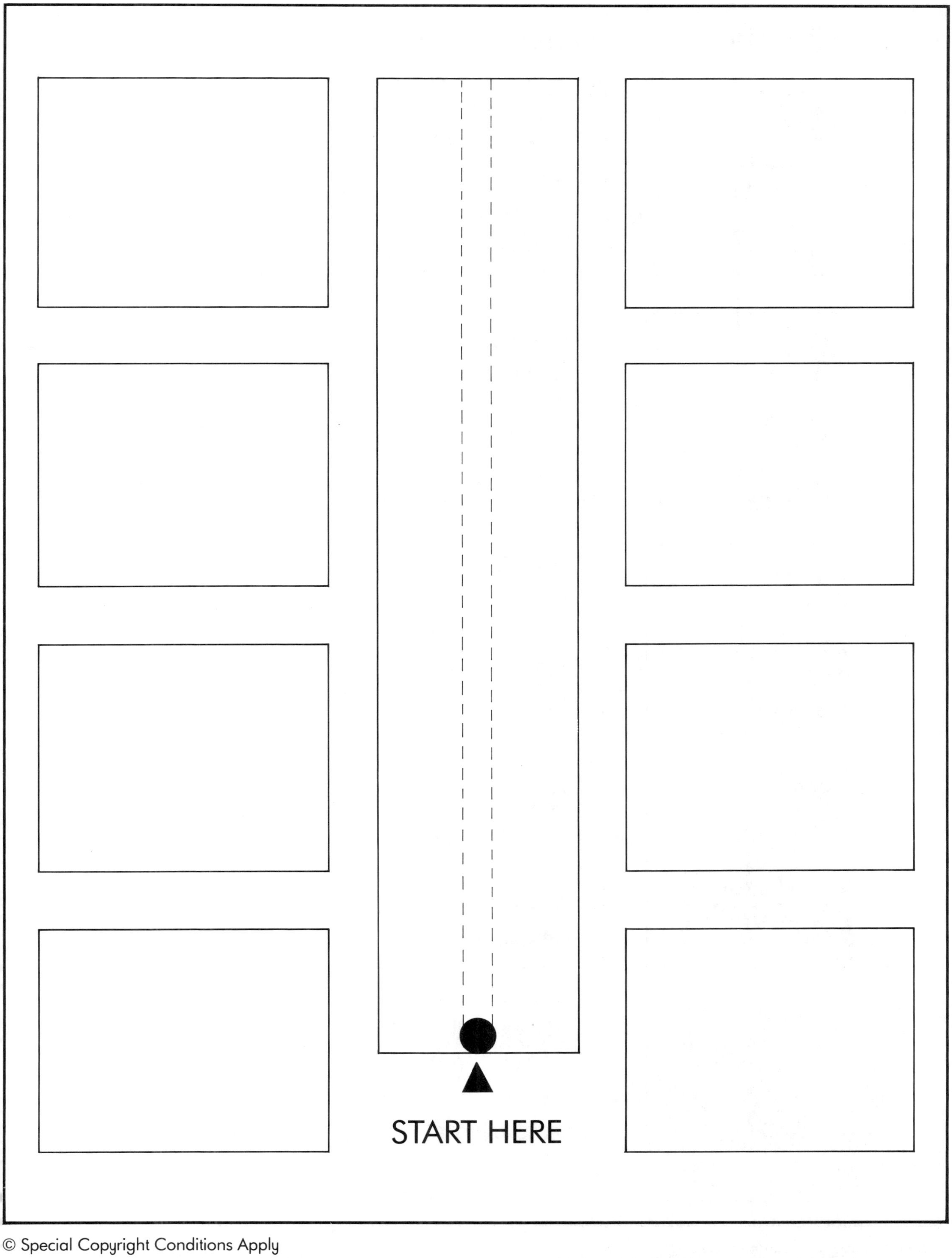

START HERE

Reasons to move

People	Reasons to move	Places to live
	Still no job! We'll have to stay here, but the baby would love a garden.	over 55s sheltered bungalow 
	I want to leave home, but I've not got much money. I need somewhere cheap to rent.	farm cottage 
	If we could sell the cottage we could buy a bigger house for us all.	big, detached house 
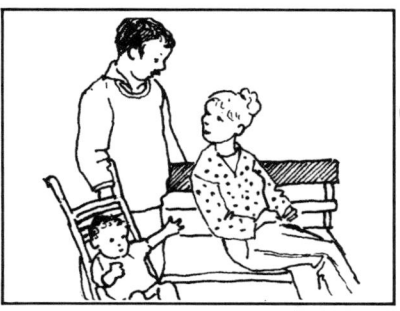	Now I'm on my own, this house is too big. I want somewhere small and safe.	flat above shop 
	If you take the job on the farm, we can live in the cottage that goes with it.	council flat 

Changing direction

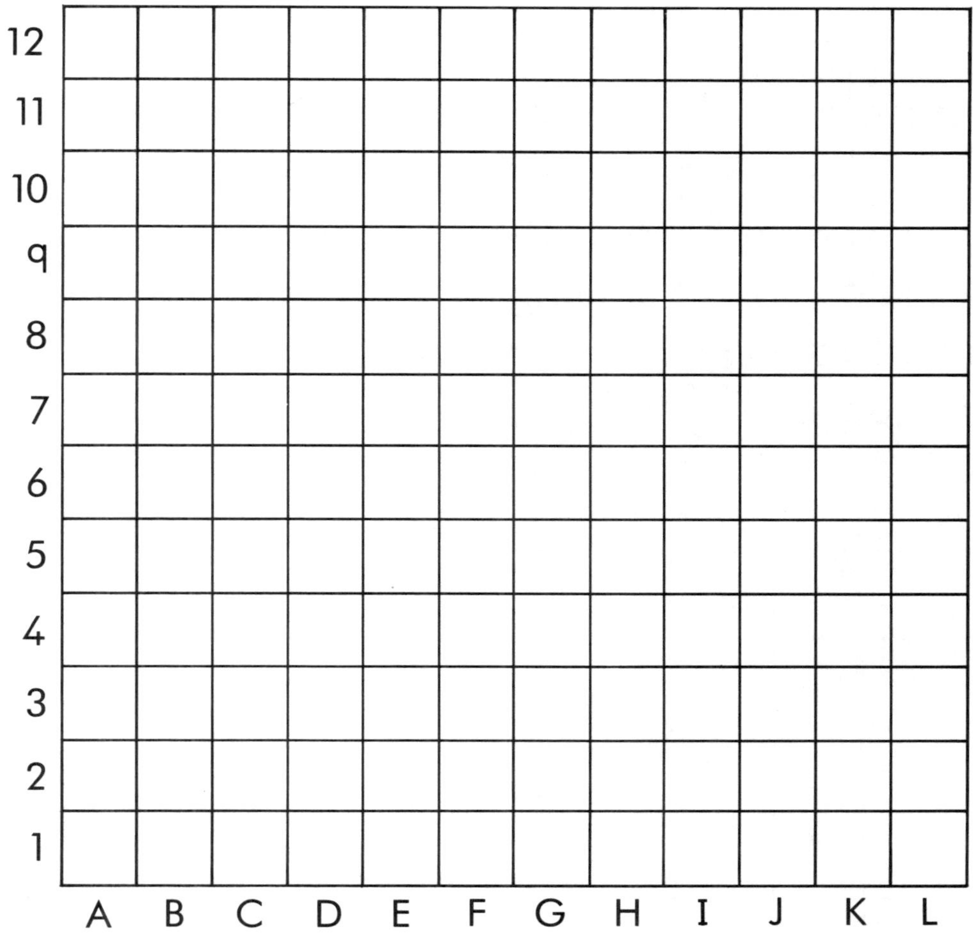

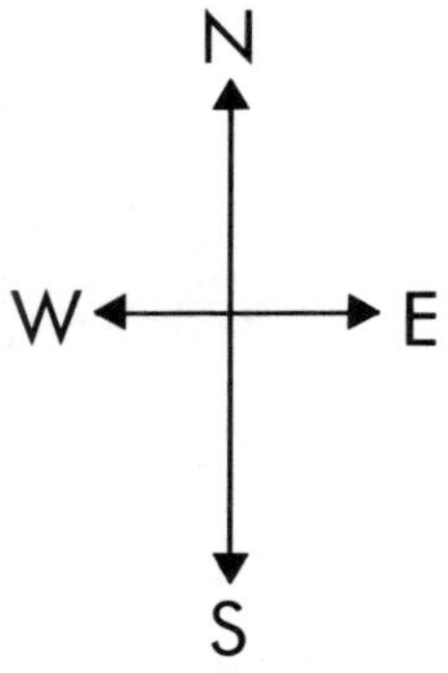

Colour the line of squares north of A1 blue.

Colour the line of squares south of L12 blue.

Colour the line of squares east of A12 blue.

Colour B11 and K11 blue.

Colour F1, G1, F2, G2, F3, G3, F4, G4, yellow.

Start at B10, go east 9 squares. Colour them red.

Start at J11, go west 7 squares. Colour them red.

Start at C7. Go north 1 square, east 1 square and south 1 square. Colour them green.

Start at I7. Go north 1 square, go east 1 square and south 1 square. Colour them green.

Start at C2. Go north 2 squares, go east 1 square and south 2 squares. Colour them green.

ACTIVITY SHEET 9

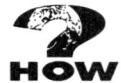

Find the houses

Work with a partner. Have one grid each, choose 6 squares to put houses on. Use the letter H to mark the squares you have chosen. Make sure your partner cannot see which you are filling in. Now take turns to guess which squares your partner has built on. Guess one square at a time.

	1	2	3	4	5	6	7	8	9	10	11	12
A												
B												
C												
D												
E												
F												
G												
H												
I												
J												
K												

ACTIVITY SHEET 10

Finding out what's there

Conwy, Wales.

Transport to and from Glasgow

Use these words and phrases to complete the diagram.
One segment has already been filled in. You may need
to use some words more than once.

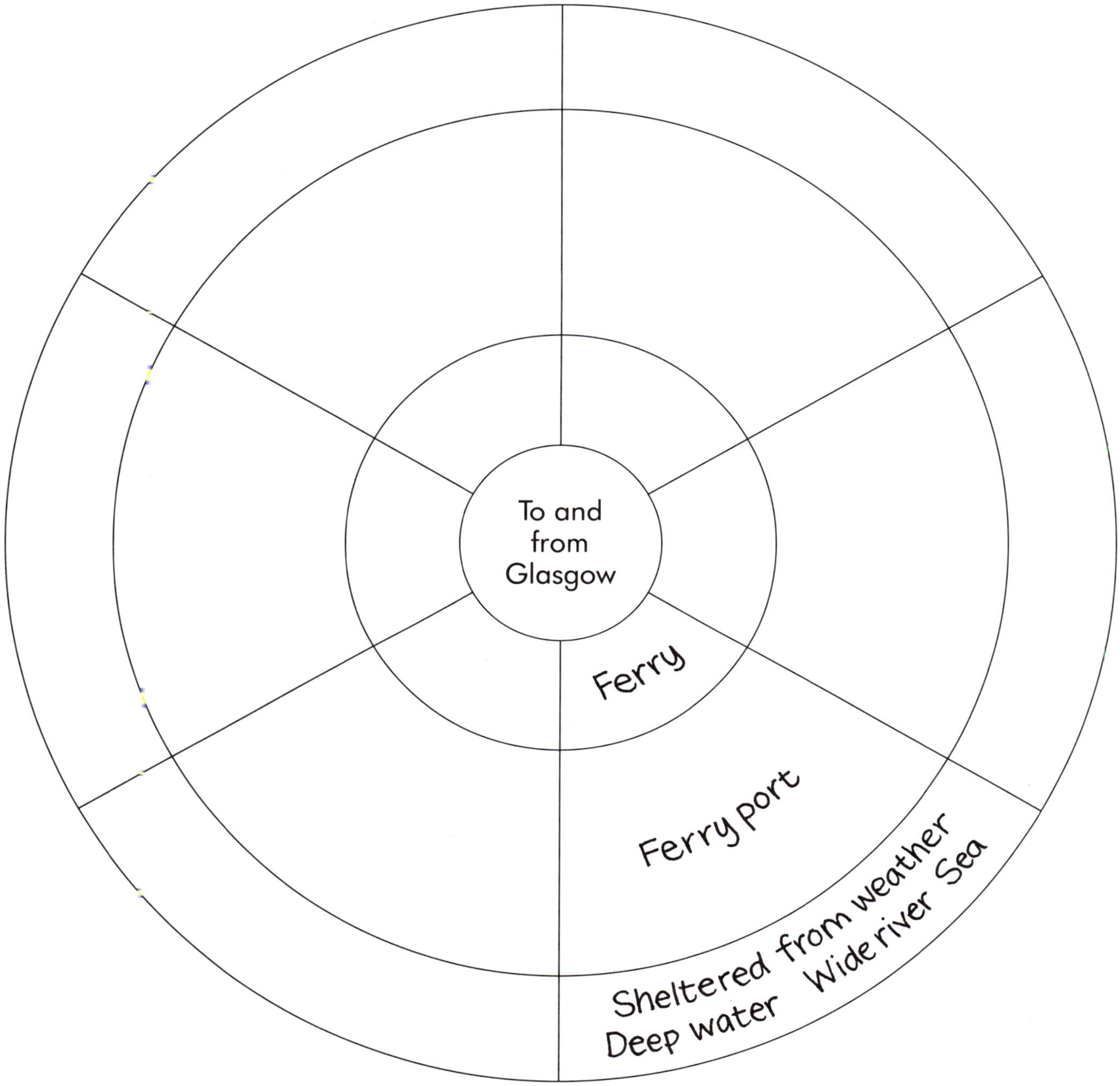

To and
from
Glasgow

Ferry

Ferry port

Sheltered from weather
Deep water   Wide river   Sea

bus

car park

large area of flat land

aeroplane

underground

land close to centre of city

car/van/lorry

flat land

land close to city centre

train

airport

station

bus station

rocky ground strong enough
to support a tunnel

Where to cross

Looking
Around

You can cross a river in many ways. Here are some of them.

a ford   a tunnel

a bridge   a ferry

Which would be the best way in each of the following situations? Write the name in the box provided.

1. The river is deep and flows fast. The banks are high and strong. A railway needs to cross.

2. The river is wide and deep and flows over strong rock. There's a huge amount of traffic and the government will provide money and machines.

3. Animals can walk through the water, tractors can drive. The river bed is not too muddy. The banks are shallow.

4. The river is wide and deep, the current is not very strong. A flat boat can take up to ten cars at a time. There is not much traffic.

Map of the United Kingdom

Key

towns/cities ○

mountain ranges △

rivers □

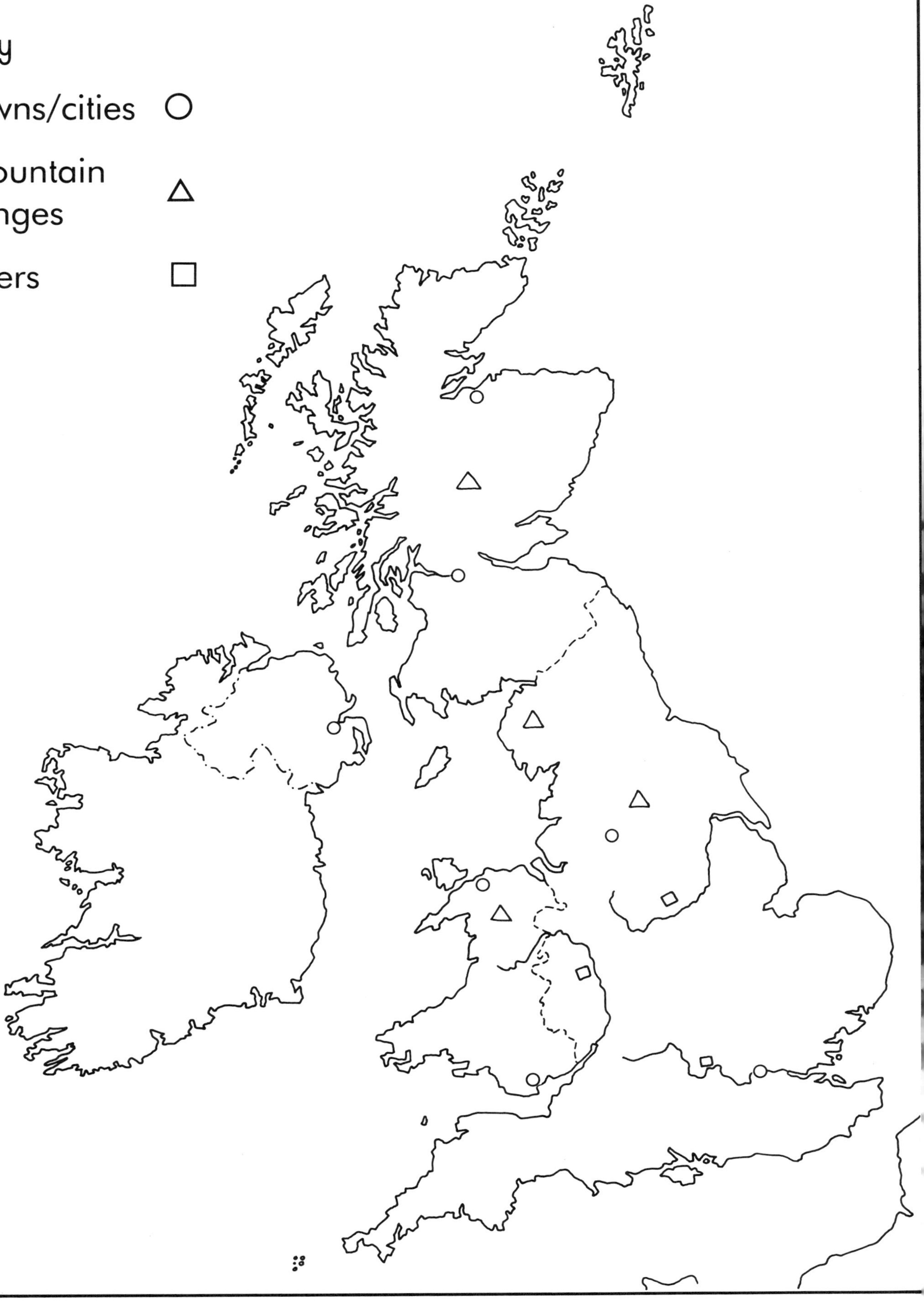

HOW

Looking
Around

Changing places

Write your answers below.

What are you doing?

Why are you doing that?

What will you use?

Is it finished?

Have you got any more plans?

Is it any good?

ACTIVITY SHEET 15

What would you add?

Add three of these to the picture. Put a tick next to those which you would like to add to your school. Put a cross next to any you do not like.

Re-Cycle BIN CANS ONLY

HOW
Looking Around

Water in the environment

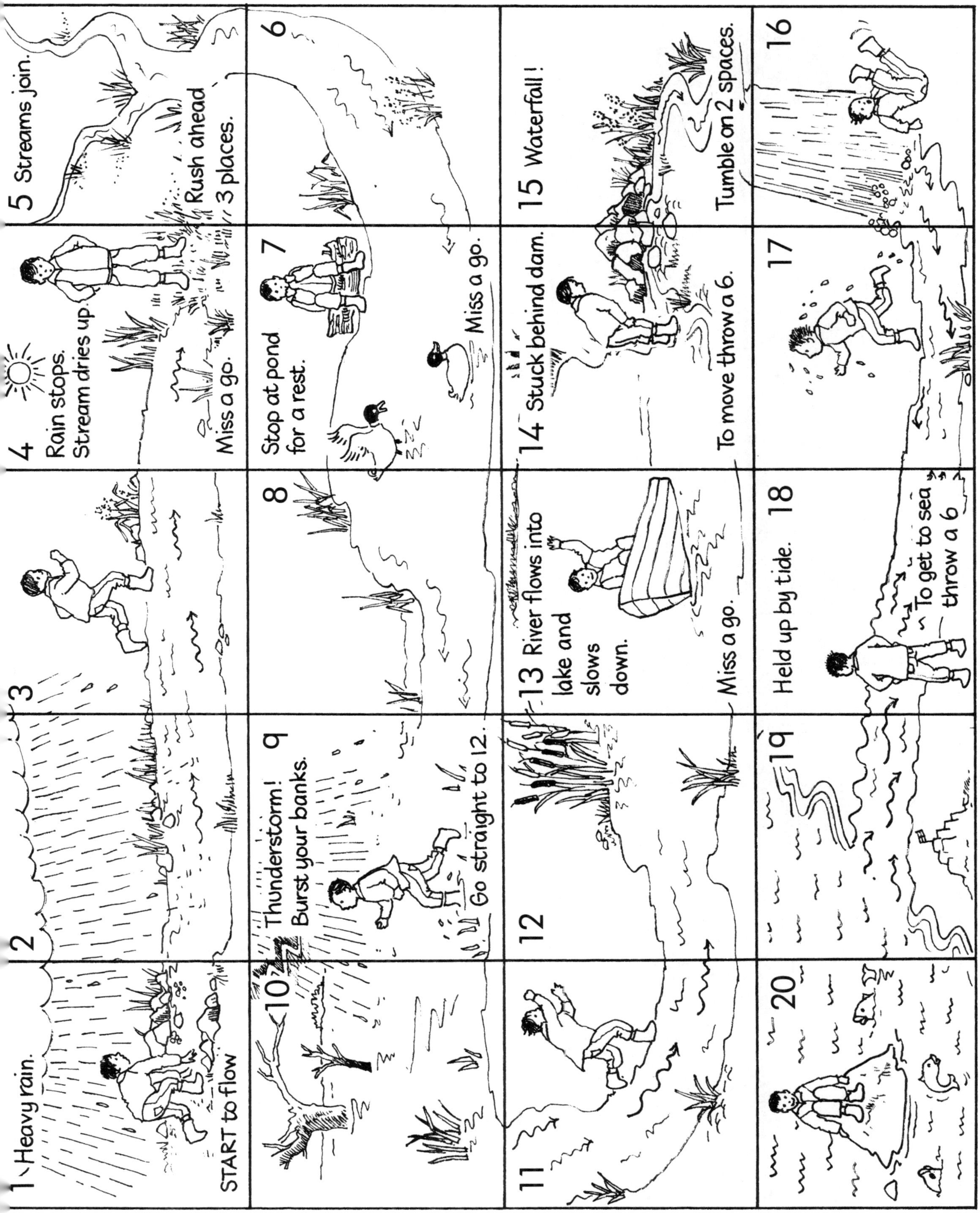

5 Streams join.
Rush ahead 3 places.

6

15 Waterfall!
Tumble on 2 spaces.

16

4 Rain stops. Stream dries up.
Miss a go.

7 Stop at pond for a rest.

Miss a go.

14 Stuck behind dam.
To move throw a 6.

17

3

8

13 River flows into lake and slows down.
Miss a go.

Held up by tide. 18

To get to sea throw a 6

2

10 Thunderstorm! Burst your banks.
Go straight to 12.

12

19

1 Heavy rain.
START to flow

9

11

20

ACTIVITY SHEET 17

Trees and Seasons cards

Tree — Autumn	Autumn
Tree — Summer	Summer
Tree — Spring	Spring
Tree — Winter	Winter

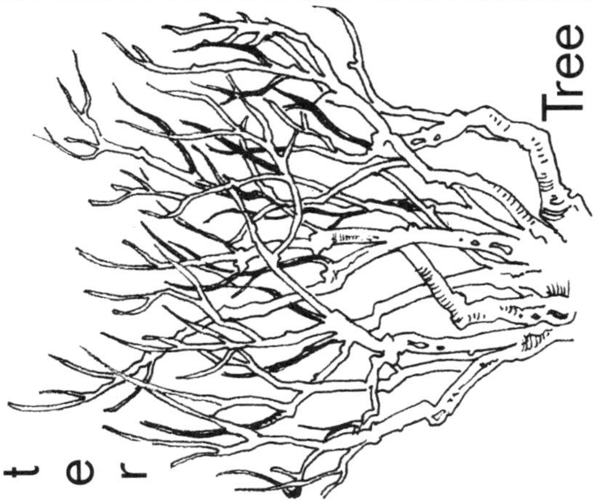

Day/Night and Clothing cards

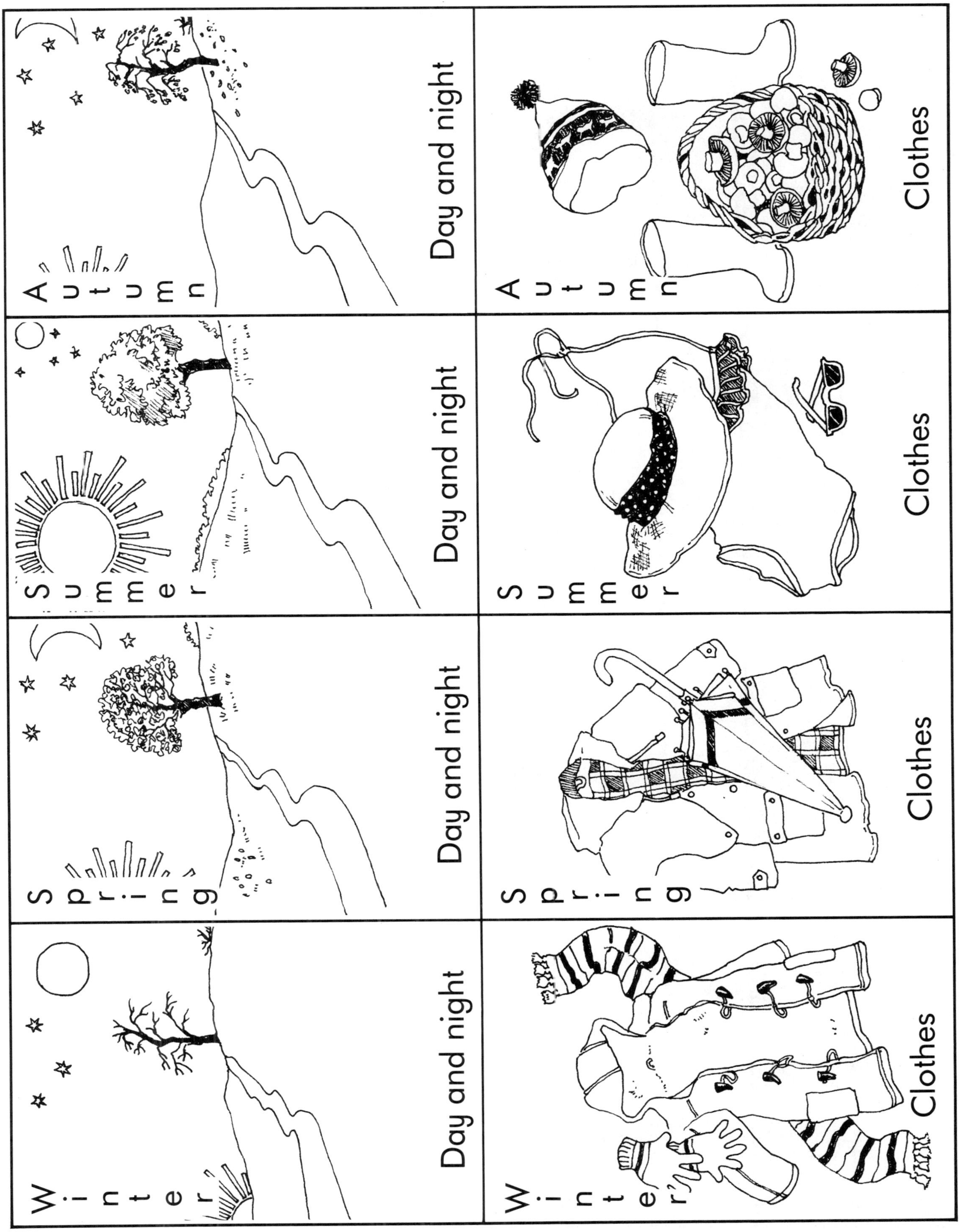

Day and night

Autumn

Clothes

Autumn

Day and night

Summer

Clothes

Summer

Day and night

Spring

Clothes

Spring

Day and night

Winter

Clothes

Winter

ACTIVITY SHEET 19

Flora and Weather cards

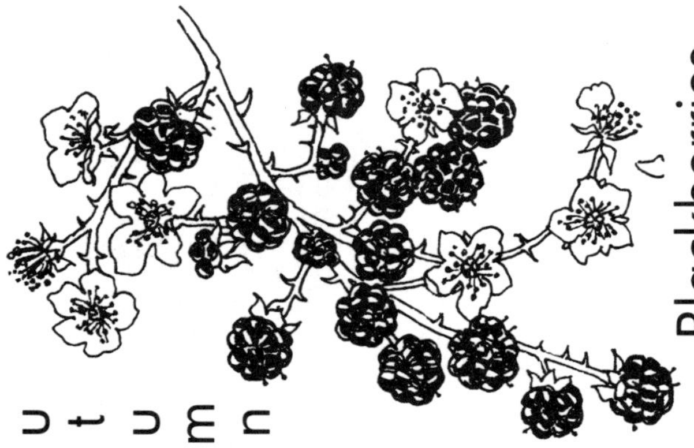

Blackberries — Autumn	Weather — Autumn
Dogrose — Summer	Weather — Summer
Dandelion — Spring	Weather — Spring
Winter jasmine — Winter	Weather — Winter

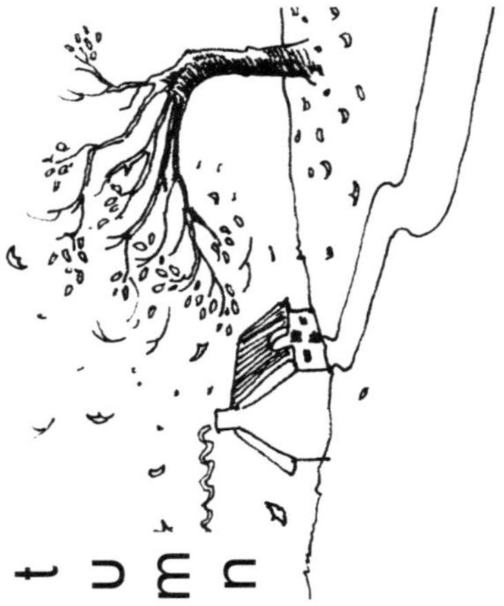

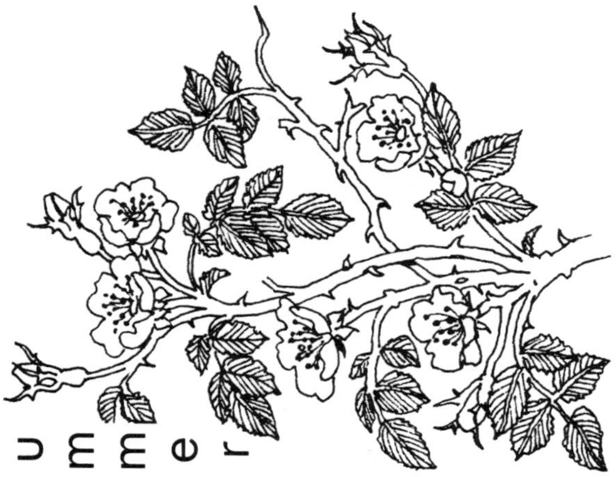

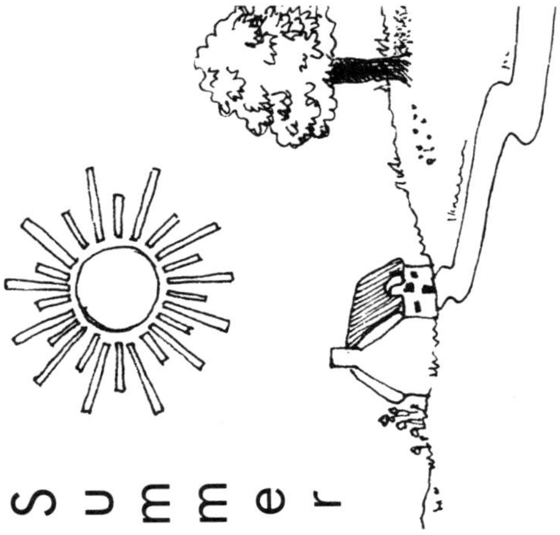

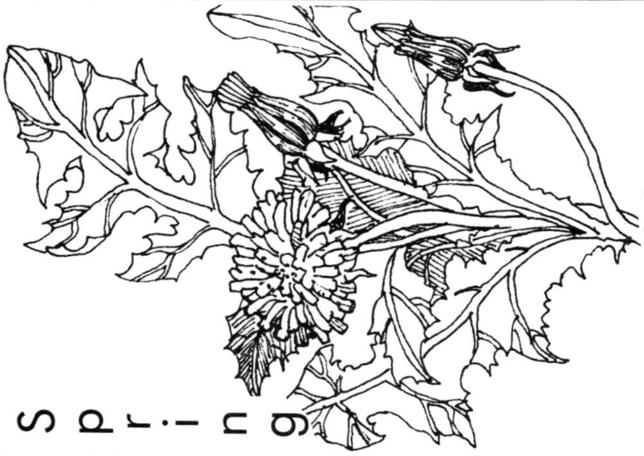

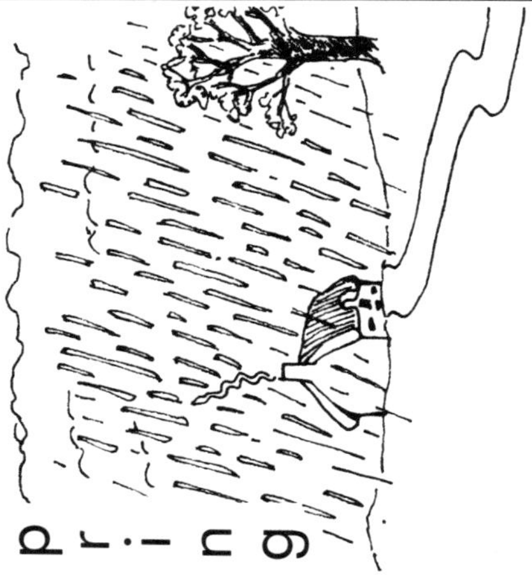

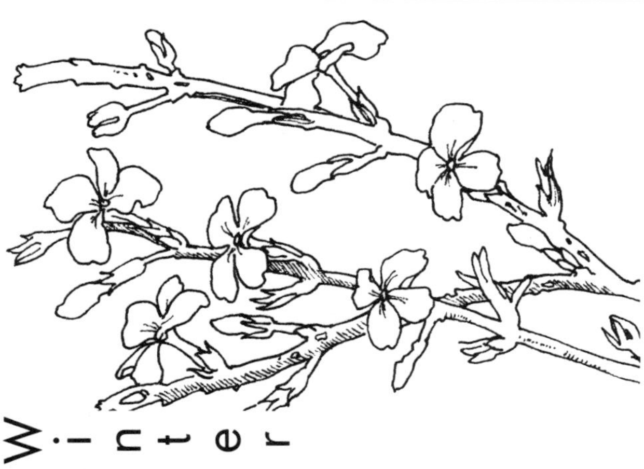

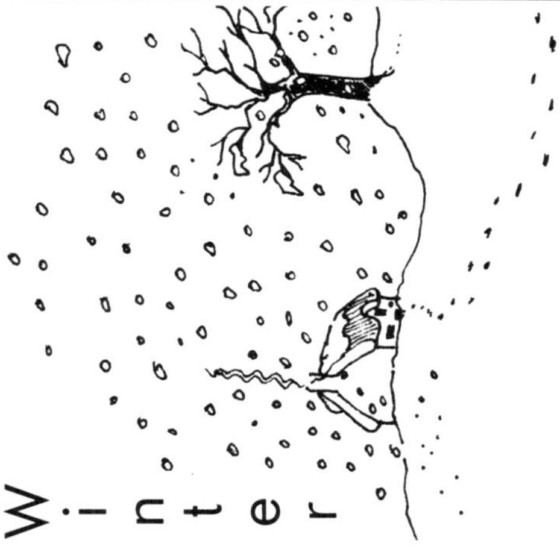

Instructions for card games

Game 1

Pelmanism.

Choose a card with one of the seasons on it. Shuffle the rest, and put them face down on the table. Now you have to collect a full set of four to match your season. The dealer goes first. Turn over a card. If it matches 'your' season, then keep it. If not, put it back face downwards. The turn lasts until you pick a losing card. The first to collect a complete set is the winner.

Game 2

This is played like Happy Families by four players.

Let all four players choose a season card. Now the dealer shuffles the rest of the pack and deals them out equally among the players. If you are the dealer, you go first. Ask the player on your left for one of the cards that goes with your season. You must name the one you want. (For example, 'Have you got some elderberries?' if you are collecting Autumn cards.)

How a thermometer works

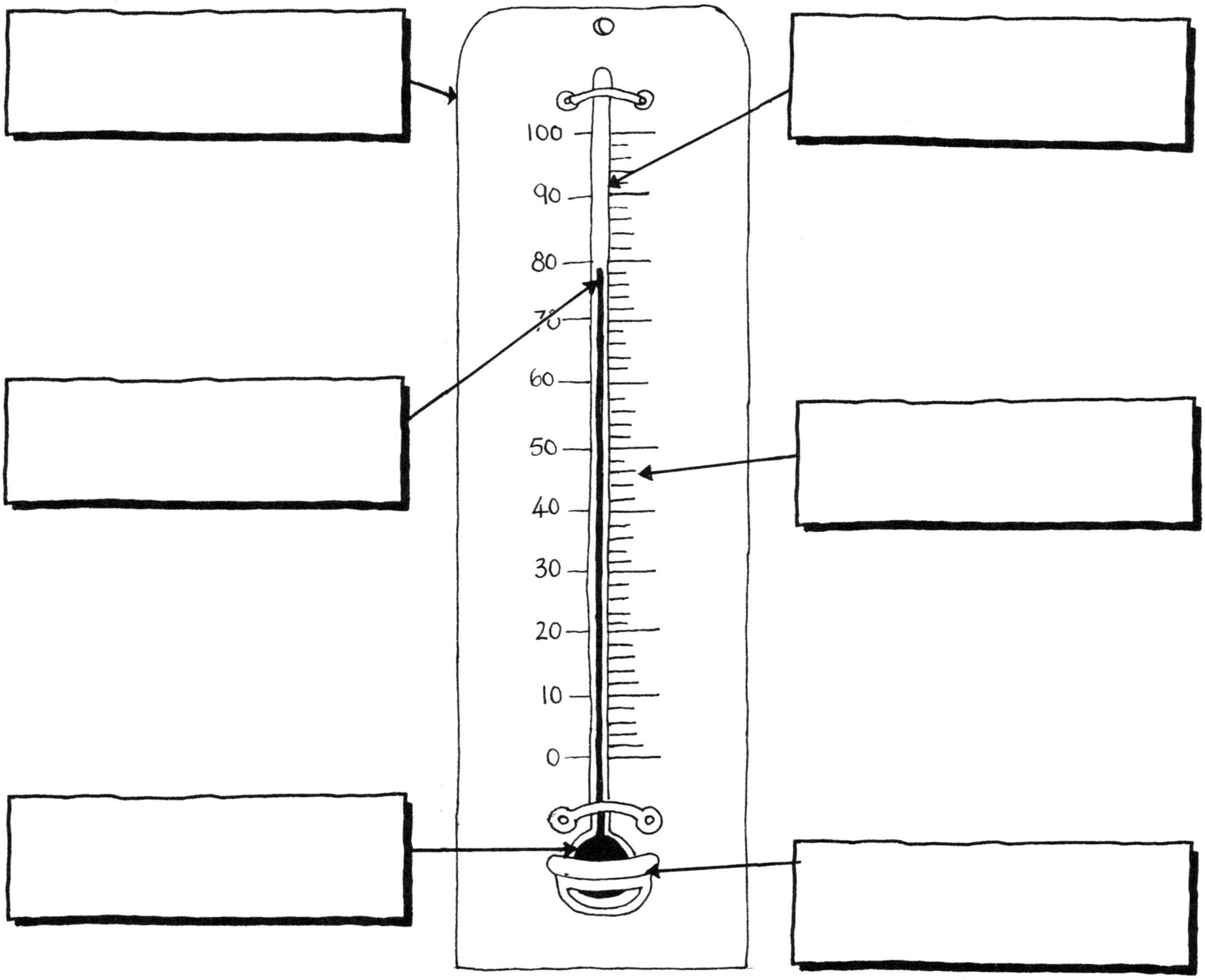

Fit the labels to the diagram of the thermometer.

Scale in degrees
centigrade

Base to hold
thermometer

Reservoir for liquid

Glass tube to hold
liquid

Guard to protect
reservoir

Liquid mercury
showing temperature

Looking
Around

The Hydrological Cycle
or What Goes Up Must Come Down

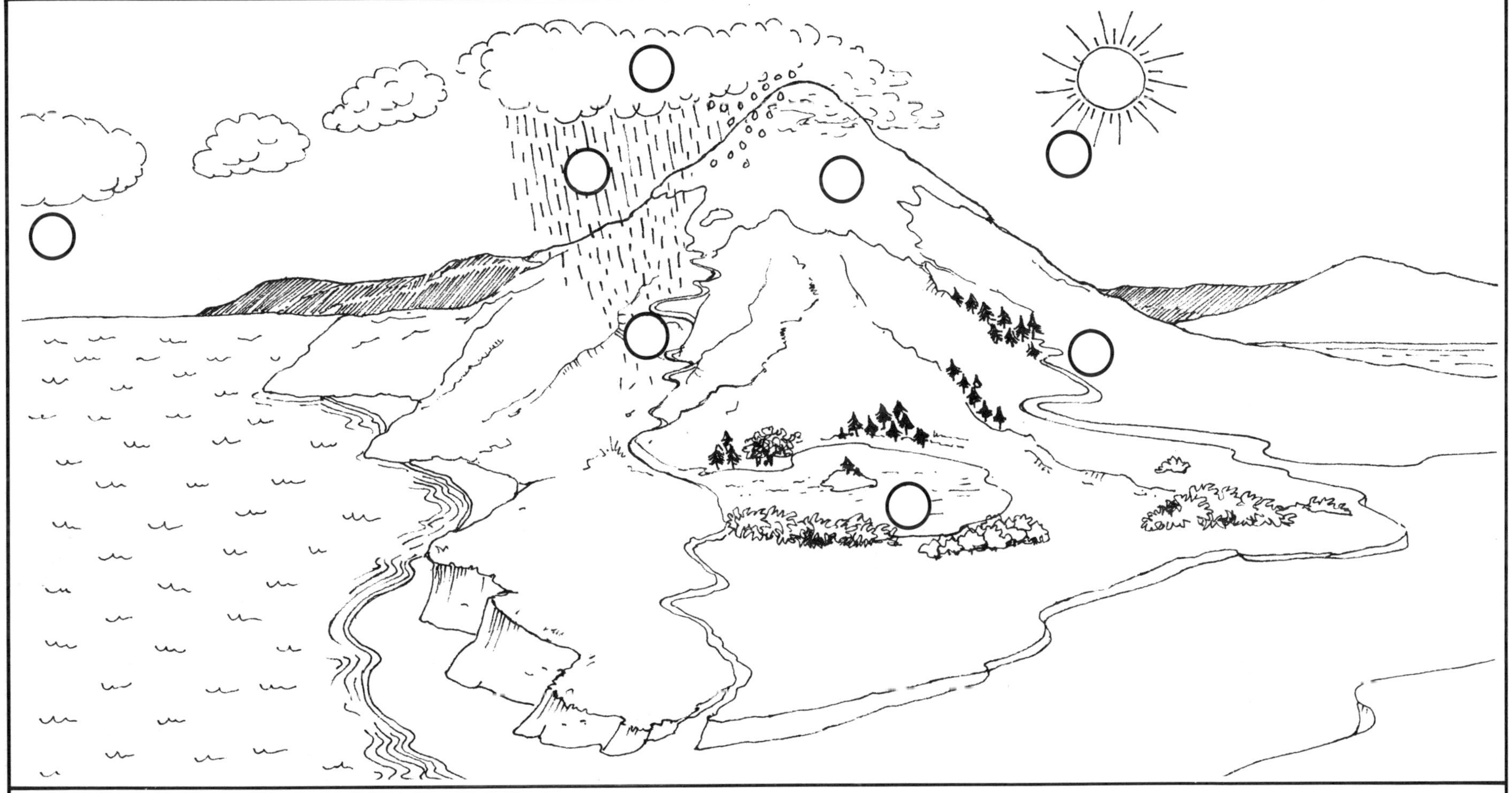

Write the caption numbers in the circles where they belong:

1 Snow melting on mountains

2 Rivers formed by snow melting

3 Rain filling rivers

4 Lake stores water between mountains and sea

5 Heat from sun evaporates water

6 Clouds formed by water vapour

7 Clouds cooled near mountains making snow, rain and mist.

HOW

Looking
Around

Weather diary

WEATHER DIARY FOR .... Date	Snow Heavy rain Showers Dry	Hot Warm Cool Cold	Windy Calm	Cloudy Sunny Mixed			
Monday							
Tuesday							
Wednesday							
Thursday							
Friday							
Saturday							
Sunday							

ACTIVITY SHEET 24

Weather symbols

Weather type	Symbol	Your symbol
CLOUD		
RAIN		
WIND		
FOG		
SUNSHINE		
THUNDER AND LIGHTNING		

Record Keeping Chart

Statement of Attainment	AT1									AT2										AT3					AT4							AT5				
	2a	2b	2c	2d	2e	3a	3b	3c	3d	2a	2b	2c	2d	3a	3b	3c	3d	3e	3f	2a	2b	3a	3b	3c	2a	2b	2c	3a	3b	3c	3d	2a	2b	2c	3a	3b
Activities in which it is addressed (Write names here)	2 3 5 7 9	2 8	3 4 6	3 18 21	2 3 5 7 9	6	21	4	7	11		1 3		3	11	11	21			14 15 16 17 19 20	13 14 15 16 17 19		13 14 15 16 17 19		10			5	8	9			12			12

Level 2 Statements not addressed in this book are covered in *People Live Here*.
Level 3 is addressed more fully in *Here and There* and *Where You Live*.

HEINEMANN OUR WORLD GEOGRAPHY TOPICS

KEY STAGE 1 (Levels 1 – 3)
Out and About
Homes and Settlements
Just Outside

LOWER KEY STAGE 2 (Levels 2 – 4)
Our Local Community
People Live Here
Looking Around
Here and There
Where You Live

UPPER KEY STAGE 2 (Levels 3 – 5)
Comparing Places
Looking At Our Environment
Living in Europe
The World Around You